FOOD & WINE LOVER'S PUZZLE & QUIZ BOOK

The Puzzle Society™

puzzlesociety.com

**Andrews McMeel
Publishing, LLC**

Kansas City • Sydney • London

09 10 11 12 13 RR2 10 9 8 7 6 5 4 3 2 1

ISBN-13: 978-0-7407-8509-2
ISBN-10: 0-7407-8509-5

Certified Chain of Custody
60% Certified Fiber Sourcing and
40% Post-Consumer Recycled
www.sfiprogram.org

SUSTAINABLE FORESTRY INITIATIVE

The SFI label only applies to the text stock.

All puzzles supplied under license from Puzzler Media Ltd.

www.puzzler.com

www.andrewsmcmeel.com

www.puzzlesociety.com

ATTENTION: SCHOOLS AND BUSINESSES
Andrews McMeel books are available at quantity discounts with bulk purchase for educational, business, or sales promotional use. For information, please write to: Special Sales Department, Andrews McMeel Publishing, LLC, 1130 Walnut Street, Kansas City, Missouri 64106.

INTRODUCTION

The *Food & Wine Lover's Puzzle & Quiz Book* contains
over 200 epicurean puzzles to challenge fanatical
foodies and test the most ravenous of puzzlers.
Crosswords, word searches, codewords, quizzes,
and many more, all with a gourmet theme.

HOW TO SOLVE

Most of the puzzles in this book do not need an explanation,
but you might find the following directions useful.

WORD SEARCH

Find the words, which are hidden in the word search grid reading
in straight lines—horizontally, vertically, or diagonally—in
either direction. Only search for words that are in CAPITAL
LETTERS. Two or more words in a phrase, like FINDERS
KEEPERS, will usually be hidden separately in the grid. Due
to limited space word search solutions are not included.

ARROWORD

Solve the puzzle by writing your answers in
the directions indicated by the arrows.

CODEWORD

Each number in the grid represents a different letter. We've given
three letters to start you off; the rest is up to you. Write these
letters wherever their corresponding numbers appear in the grid
and then begin to work out the identity of the other letters.
All 26 letters of the alphabet will appear in the finished grid.

1 CROSSWORD

Rearrange the letters in the shaded squares to spell out a dessert (5,5).

ACROSS

7 Dairy food for spreading on bread (6)

8 Slip-ups (6)

9 With the addition of (4)

10 Coastal resort in southern Mexico (8)

11 Popular vegetable with hamburgers (6,5)

14 Richard Rodgers's musical partner (11)

18 Hard dry cheese from northern Italy (8)

19 Is situated or located (4)

20 Chilled creamy dessert (6)

21 Give (someone) the latest news (6)

DOWN

1 Knives, forks, and spoons (7)

2 ___ Redding, "My Girl" singer (4)

3 Deliver a sermon (6)

4 Place near Hollywood (3,3)

5 Quarrel (8)

6 Fool, dupe (5)

12 Narrowly avoided collision (4,4)

13 Statue of ___, New York landmark (7)

15 Edible marine creature with an elongated oval shell (6)

16 Expired (3,3)

17 Conductor's wand (5)

19 Lord's wife (4)

BAKE
BARBECUE
BLANCHE
BOIL
BRAISE
BROWN
CODDLE
DEEP-FRY
GRILL
MICROWAVE
PICKLE
POACH
REDUCE
REHEAT
ROAST
SAUTE
SCRAMBLE
SIMMER
STEAM
STEW
STIR-FRY
TENDER
THICKEN
TOAST

```
B  R  A  I  S  E  R  D  E  X  P  W  Z  M  O
E  A  M  P  B  N  E  D  E  H  T  W  E  A  R
L  Y  R  A  O  E  C  A  V  B  C  L  E  E  I
K  K  K  B  P  A  S  F  A  Q  D  N  H  T  L
C  E  H  F  E  U  C  N  W  D  J  E  A  S  S
I  V  R  G  S  C  W  H  O  E  A  R  X  L  P
P  Y  W  Z  C  O  U  C  R  T  O  M  N  D  B
T  S  A  O  R  T  Y  E  C  C  A  B  I  R  N
S  K  S  B  A  F  S  T  I  R  F  R  Y  E  T
E  I  Q  L  M  H  U  J  M  V  G  E  K  D  O
R  T  M  X  B  R  E  D  N  E  T  C  P  U  A
W  Z  U  M  L  I  O  B  O  M  I  N  D  C  S
T  Y  C  A  E  A  B  I  K  H  S  F  Q  E  T
L  H  U  J  S  R  V  G  T  E  G  R  I  L  L
```

3 ARROWORD

The arrows show the direction in which the answer to each clue should be placed. When complete, rearrange the shaded squares to spell out a type of grape used to make wine.

Design of buildings	▼	__ Thurman, actress	▼	Ever-hopeful person	Loved one	Lose vital fluid	▼
Form again ▶				▼	▼		
For what reason?		Chimpanzee, e.g. ▶				Parts of a chair	
▶			Story ▶			▼	
Took food		Discharged (a gun) ▶					
▶			Mixture of different styles		Book lover		Half of forty
Impeach		In a winning position? ▶	▼		▼		▼
▶						Gone with the Wind mansion	
__ Dench, M in James Bond films		Ohio or Florida, e.g. ▶				▼	
▶			__ Brown, The Da Vinci Code author ▶				
Gas used for advertising signs		For all to see ▶					
▶			Jamie Foxx film ▶				

4 PATHFINDER

Beginning with the C in the square box, follow a continuous path to find 23 soft drinks. The trail passes through each and every letter once, and may twist up, down, or sideways, but never diagonally.

C	S	H	A	S	U	I	S	T	R	A	I	N
R	U	S	T	S	N	K	R	C	O	N	G	A
D	N	U	H	A	L	A	Y	E	S	E	I	M
R	H	I	S	I	L	T	S	P	P	S	X	O
O	E	A	I	G	U	N	H	W	E	E	V	E
P	N	N	I	H	O	T	C	S	D	E	R	N
H	C	P	A	T	C	R	Y	T	I	I	G	U
M	N	U	W	A	H	D	O	O	M	B	E	P
O	T	R	I	T	E	R	O	H	E	S	C	P
U	E	Y	A	F	R	P	O	C	A	L	I	E
N	I	G	W	S	E	E	Y	O	C	O	C	P
T	D	O	E	Q	P	P	A	L	A	P	I	S
A	I	N	D	U	I	R	T	S	N	P	L	E

BIG RED	HAWAIIAN PUNCH	SHASTA
COCA-COLA	MOUNTAIN DEW	SLICE
COUNTRY TIME	MOXIE	SNAPPLE
CRUSH	NEHI	SQUIRT
CRYSTAL LIGHT	ORANGINA	SUN DROP
DIET RITE	PEPSI	SUNKIST
DR PEPPER	SCHWEPPES	YOO-HOO
FAYGO	SEVEN UP	

5 CODEWORD

In this crossword, each letter of the alphabet appears as a code number. When you have replaced the decoded numbers with their letters in the grid, fill in the boxes at the bottom to reveal a saying or phrase.

10	15	26	10	15	17	2		2	11	17	23	12
25		22		22		22	9	25		5		22
25	10 **R**	13 **B**	6 **I**	14	22	24		19	22	11	24	17
26		10		17		26	15	15		6		2
17	23	6	17		17			24	22	13		19
		4	2	6	15	26	24	12		17	1	22
10			12		20		25		8			23
15	24	19		1	22	16	22	19	22	17		
3		6	4	15			18		21	25	7	15
6		20		10	25	13		17		24		22
17	14	15	22	19		15	10	22	17	15	10	17
15		10		15	15	24		9		19		15
21	25	17	15	21		24	15	22	10	18	15	21

A B̸ C D E F G H̸ I̸ J K L M N O P Q R̸ S T U V W X Y Z

1	2	3	4	5	6 **I**	7	8	9	10 **R**	11	12	13 **B**
14	15	16	17	18	19	20	21	22	23	24	25	26

THE SAYING OR PHRASE IS:

22	19	15	10	6	4	22	18		22	17

22	1	1	24	15		1	6	15

WINE LIST

ALICANTE

ALMANSA

ALSACE

ANJOU

ASTI SPUMANTE

BARBARESCO

BARDOLINO

BEAUJOLAIS

BORDEAUX

BURGUNDY

CABERNET

CARINENA

CHABLIS

CHAMPAGNE

CHARDONNAY

CHIANTI

CHINON

COLOMBARD

COTE de
   BEAUNE

FRASCATI

GEWURZTRAMINER

GRENACHE

GRIGNOLINO

HERMITAGE

JEREZ

LAMBRUSCO

LOIRE

LUDON

MACONNAIS

MARGAUX

MEDOC

MERLOT

MUSCADET

PAUILLAC

PIEDMONT

PINOT NOIR

POMEROL

RHONE VALLEY

RIBEIRO

RIESLING

RIOJA

SANCERRE

SANGIOVESE

SAUMUR

SAUTERNES

SAUVIGNON
   BLANC

SEMILLON

SHIRAZ

SOAVE

SYLVANER

SYRAH

TEMPRANILLO

TREBBIANO

VALENCIA

VALPOLICELLA

VERDEJO

VERDICCHIO

ZINFANDEL

✽ Only search for words that are
in CAPITAL LETTERS. Two or
more words in a phrase, like
FINDERS KEEPERS, will usually be
hidden separately in the grid.

```
O E T O C Z G V X Y S A U M U R A V B P P
E L I G R B A R D O L I N O P S E N O X E
N E L H I L C N I L T T N A C R F M J G U
U T O I L A U H E G N N U O D J E O A O E
A N I E N G L C A I N I O I N R E T D X U
E A R O R A I O H B L O C M O I I D Z U S
B M S U R L R C J L L C L L D M H E R A L
L U B T O I G P A U H I N I R E R C U E E
A P K P Y O E C M I A T S E N E I T M D V
N S L C Y J W B O E S E H Y J O E P U R A
A A M O A E U F I A T A B C L R S S S O L
V D E L N D R I A R I H S S N V A O C B L
L U D O N R Z C A B E R N E T U A O A E E
O G O M O E T Z A M U P S S M P W N D V Y
U R B B D V R S I A L O J U A E B N E T E
C J B A R B A R E S C O H E R N A N T O C
W H H R A R M S A E E I O I T F C O D E M
H T A W H V I S H M S N O C N N C E J Z S
L E R M C O N E Q I E L O I S I A L R Y I
L M Y P P A E N S L V Q Z M P U F C L R K
E P S D M A R C O L O M B A R D R V I M E
C R C L A U G I H O I N O I Q O A B R L N
I A A T C R A N O I G N O V N N S S M O A
L N R I O J A S E L N V A O E A C Y I A M
O I I I N E C A S L A O L R C I A R F D L
P L N O N G I V U A S L S B T B T A U C M
L L E A A E G Y A R I H S L M B I D A N A
A A N L I T N R T M E H C A N E R G E E R
V W C A S L A A E O I B O N H R R V D L G
I T N A I H C S J R N O X C O T K L R A A
A I C N E L A V A R R I E S L I N G O V U
C H A B L I Y Z C H A M P A G N U E B T X
```

7 CROSSWORD

Rearrange the letters in the shaded squares to spell out a type of wine.

ACROSS

7 Chinese sugar-vinegar sauce (5-3-4)
8 "The Last Frontier" state (6)
9 Flour grain (5)
10 Accompanied, waited upon (8)
13 Knock (into) (4)
15 Outer border (4)
16 Putting off for a while (8)
17 From the biggest continent (5)
19 Items of historic interest (6)
21 Fast-food meal in a bun (12)

DOWN

1 Kept separate, quarantined (8)
2 Florida islets (4)
3 Left helpless (8)
4 Chew away at (4)
5 Legislative body (8)
6 Impartial (4)
11 Cosmetic pencil (8)
12 Feverishness, hysteria (8)
14 Care of the fingernails (8)
17 Prolonged pain (4)
18 Have to have (4)
20 Journey stages (4)

8 FOOD QUIZ

1 What is the oldest restaurant in Boston?

2 What is the British term for "shrimp"?

3 What type of vegetable is a butternut?

4 Which nuts are used to make marzipan?

5 Apart from lemons, what else is used to make lemon curd?

6 Why is eating bran good for your health, and how is bran obtained?

7 What is the main vegetable ingredient of borscht?

8 How many calories are in a medium-size egg?

CODEWORD

In this crossword, each letter of the alphabet appears as a code number. When you have replaced the decoded numbers with their letters in the grid, fill in the boxes at the bottom to reveal a saying or phrase.

25	1	24	16	13	25	4	24	■	19	24	15	4
6	■	6	■	26	■	25	■	10	■	12	■	24
11	21	3	24	18	■	4	2	20	3	11 **I**	9	15
23	■	18	■	22	■	4	■	2	■	9 **C**	■	4
26	2	20	26	■	9	20	23	10	24	4 **T**	4	11
■	■	11	■	14	■	20	■	24	■	■	■	10
1	13	4	11	24	15	■	3	11	26	15	4	22
13	■	■	■	8	■	12	■	4	■	4	■	■
2	20	25	1	15	17	20	14	■	7	11	23	9
25	■	21	■	11	■	20	■	25	■	21	■	18
8	20	25	15	4	24	1	■	15	25	13	23	25
18	■	7	■	24	■	20	■	5	■	18	■	23
24	22	24	1	■	8	20	20	15	4	11	23	26

A B C̸ D E F G H I̸ J K L M N O P Q R S T̸ U V W X Y Z

1	2	3	4 **T**	5	6	7	8	9 **C**	10	11 **I**	12	13
14	15	16	17	18	19	20	21	22	23	24	25	26

THE SAYING OR PHRASE IS:

25	9	17	11	3		20	23	4	17	24

	15	17	20	13	18	1	24	2

10 ARROWORD

The arrows show the direction in which the answer to each clue should be placed. When complete, rearrange the letters in the shaded squares to spell out a brand of beer.

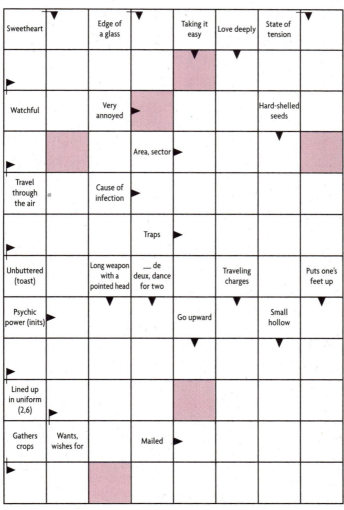

BILL
BISTRO
CAFE
CHEF
COFFEE
CUTLERY
DESSERT
DINING OUT
EATERY
ITALIAN
KITCHEN
MAIN COURSE
MEAL
MENU
MINTS
PLATE
RESTAURANT
SERVICE
SIDE SALAD
STARTER

```
S T M I A W W E A T R I
T N A I L A T I S W E N
E L N U N I O I K P T O
A T L C N T D U I I R I
K U A U U E S T T O A T
H R E T B R M C C R T A
O E M L A T U K H T S V
U S S E R V I C E S N R
S T E R N G N I N I D E
E A S Y U I H O A B F S
A U A A N O W M Y R E E
I R L L I B C R T A H R
L A A I N E E F F O C V
I N D L S T R E S S E D
C T P L A T E L E R R A
C A F E L B A T R M E A
```

STEAKHOUSE
TABLE RESERVATION

TIP
WAITER
WINE BAR

✱ Two or more words in a phrase, like FINDERS KEEPERS, will usually be hidden
separately in the grid.

12 **FRUIT FULL**

Can you fit the ten jigsaw pieces in the grid so that the name of a fruit or vegetable appears down each of the seven columns?

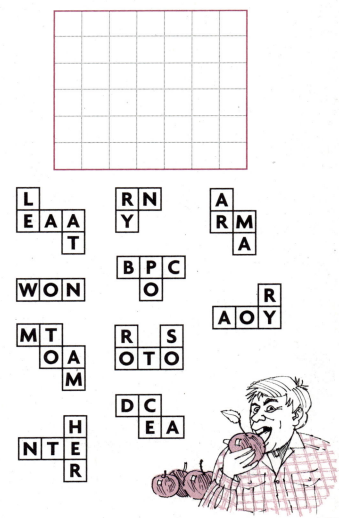

Add a letter to each of the words so that they fit the clue. The added letters will spell an item of food.

SOCK		Basis of soup
PEST		Sauce for pasta
GAPE		Fruit
ART		Flan, cake
SCAMP		Shrimp dish
BOW		Food basin
FAVOR		Taste
MET		Food from an animal

14 **FOOD FACTS**

- Tootsie Rolls were the first wrapped penny candy in America.

- The pineapple is a sign of hospitality.

- Massachusetts' state beverage is cranberry juice.

- Honey is the only food that does not spoil.

- Black-eyed peas are not peas; they are beans.

- Horseradish was the first of the HJ Heinz 57 varieties.

- More people are killed each year by falling coconuts than by shark attacks.

- If an egg floats, it means it is rotten.

15 CROSSWORD

Rearrange the letters in the shaded squares to spell out a breakfast food.

ACROSS

8 Wear away chemically (7)
9 Courtroom plea of being elsewhere (5)
10 Sour-tasting yellow fruit (5)
11 Mexican filled tortilla (7)
12 Subtext (12)
16 Portable two-way radio (6-6)
20 Afternoon performance (7)
23 Vehicle's steering device (5)
24 Choose (by ballot) (5)
25 Place where a train stops (7)

DOWN

1 Burn with liquid (5)
2 Felon (8)
3 Recline casually and comfortably (6)
4 Plant used to flavor cooking (4)
5 More equitable (6)
6 South Pacific island group (4)
7 Italian rice dish (7)
13 Feline creature (3)
14 Outbreak of infectious disease (8)
15 Person moving through water (7)
17 Set fire to (6)
18 Police officer (6)
19 Unable to see (5)
21 Bound with string (4)
22 Far from difficult (4)

```
N N O M M I S R E P A P
T A U C H E R R Y Q T R
C L E M E N T I N E A S
P R N T T E E L W E U P
H E A T O C I R P A Q W
E D A A B T N I E G M E
G F E C C A N R M R U A
N A N I H R N O I A K B
A X P I F I G A L P M E
R S W P A N A U N E L P
O I E R L E O G N A M T
K E N I R E G N A T A N
```

APPLE

APRICOT

BANANA

CHERRY

CLEMENTINE

DATE

FIG

GRAPE

KIWI

KUMQUAT

LIME

MANGO

MELON

NECTARINE

ORANGE

PEACH

PEAR

PERSIMMON

PLUM

TANGERINE

See how quickly you can fit the listed words into the interlocking grid. The shaded squares will reveal the name of a spice.

4 LETTERS

EDGY
FIFE

5 LETTERS

FOCUS
HOSTA
KNOLE
LATHE
OILED
SWING

6 LETTERS

HYPHEN
PARENT
THESIS
UNTIED

7 LETTERS

HANDLES
IMITATE
INCENSE
NASTILY
NITRATE
PRAYING
STAMINA
TASTIER

12 LETTERS

FAITHFULNESS
MULTITASKING
RELENTLESSLY
UNWAVERINGLY

18 **SIX-PACK**

Fit the six listed words into the pattern of adjoining hexagons. Each word may start from any triangle in its hexagon, but must be written clockwise. Adjoining triangles of adjacent hexagons must contain the same letter as each other.

BUTTER

CHEESE

NUTMEG

SHRIMP

FENNEL

ENDIVE

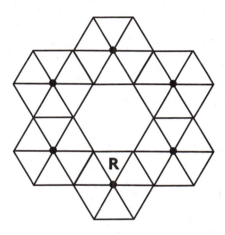

19 **WHODUNNIT?**

The murderer, the weapon used, and the area in which the crime was committed are all in the word lists but missing from the grid. Can you solve the mystery?

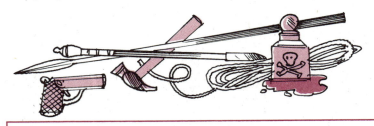

```
N V F L E H S P B X F S T A C K E R
E R E G A N A M I P A S H O N A R E
S I C G N C U E H P O U H I A G I P
S C A C H E C K O U T I F E L U W P
E I P Y E T E E U D F E S R L E E O
T Y S V A T I A P A R F U O G L S H
A R O C E D U I R R U I M T N S E S
C I D R A A R T G N I V R A C I E Y
I S B S L K X U V E T C U E G A H I
L E C O I E I E T G N N I G U N C U
E L T T O B D F P A R K I N G I U N
D S M O O R K C O T S N U C G T E S
```

DELROY of the DELICATESSEN	CARVING KNIFE	AISLE
MAGNUS the MANAGER	CHEESEWIRE	CHECK-OUT
SADIE the SATURDAY EXTRA	POISON	ENTRANCE
SHELLEY the SHELF STACKER	PRICING GUN	FRUIT & VEG
SHONA the SHOPPER	SAUCE BOTTLE	PARKING SPACE
TILDA at the TILL	STRING BAG	STOCKROOM

✳ Only search for words that are in CAPITAL LETTERS. Two or more words in a phrase, like FINDERS KEEPERS, will usually be hidden separately in the grid.

20 CODEWORD

In this crossword, each letter of the alphabet appears as a code number. When you have replaced the decoded numbers with their letters in the grid, fill in the boxes at the bottom to reveal a saying or phrase.

	12		14		10		12		23		26	
16	6	5	8	3	15		17	23	11	12	24	17
	19		11		22		11		21		11	
17	13	11	3		26	4	8	2	11	19	13	15
	6				1		18		15		12	
26	11	3	11	9	17	8	15	1	11	10		
	23		23						4		17	
	11	24	24	5	15	11	4	8	11	15	3	
	12		17		8		26				7	
2	19	4	8	3	6	18	17		12	24	5	17
	4		17		12 B		12		4		11	
2	4	15	15	11	24 L	4	8	25	6	19	23	
	23		15		17 E		20		15		17	

A B̶ C D E̶ F G H I J K L̶ M N O P Q R S T U V W X Y Z

1	2	3	4	5	6	7	8	9	10	11	12 B	13
14	15	16	17 E	18	19	20	21	22	23	24 L	25	26

THE SAYING OR PHRASE IS:

26	19	22		4	21	17	19		15	10	11	24	3

13	11	24	14

CROSSWORD

Rearrange the letters in the shaded squares to spell out a chicken dish (7,5).

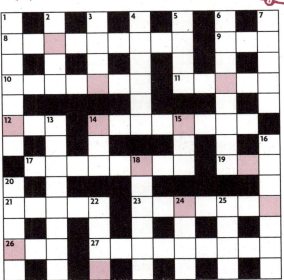

ACROSS

- **8** Building used by a sports society (9)
- **9** Domestic animal (3)
- **10** Alcoholic drink of a burgundy color (3,4)
- **11** Small open-fronted shop (5)
- **12** Male title (3)
- **14** Chocolate cakes (8)
- **17** Openly (8)
- **19** Number of shoes in a pair (3)
- **21** Atlantic or Pacific, e.g. (5)
- **23** Rocket launch (4-3)
- **26** Creative skill (3)
- **27** Exactly the same (9)

DOWN

- **1** Female film star (7)
- **2** Money source (4)
- **3** Popular Far Eastern cuisine (4)
- **4** Dinner jacket (6)
- **5** Security breach (4)
- **6** Enemy (8)
- **7** Post (5)
- **13** Gambling game using a numbered wheel (8)
- **14** Drinks counter (3)
- **15** Negating word (3)
- **16** Egg-based fluffy dish (7)
- **18** ___ wedding, 50th anniversary (6)
- **20** Devoted (5)
- **22** Metal fastener (4)
- **24** Divine will (4)
- **25** In the past (4)

1 If a cooked soup or stew tastes too salty, what can you do to rectify this?

2 Taramasalata is a Greek paste. From what kind of fish is it made?

3 What is Garfield's favorite food?

4 Bel Paese is a type of what?

5 Do eggs contain fat?

6 The vegetable okra can have other names; what are they?

7 Is the trout a freshwater or saltwater fish?

8 What is the other name for pecan nuts?

23 VOWEL PLAY

Can you replace the missing vowels to complete the names of these vegetables?

1 **C R R T**

2 **P T T**

3 **L T T C**

4 **P**

5 **L K**

6 **K L**

7 **N N**

8 **C L R Y**

9 **R D S H**

10 **B T**

```
C C S Z E C S S N W A R P S
W S A T A Y E P T B E A N M
O R Z N U A O I R O L O E D
H E I E W N U S O I O I U C
C S S E C K C B L D N H E E
C H E P C H M I L L N G S S
R D I A N A U E T A O D W E
I I L C B T S A E A X R E N
S B C E K O R H N L M U E O
P S E E S E N E E S O O T T
Y F P D B R N C G W I S R N
I E U A I O H U G N I K C A
S C P L R O A A D E I R F C
K L A I C E P S A E H G O L
```

AROMATIC DUCK

BAMBOO SHOOTS

BEEF

BLACK BEAN SAUCE

CANTONESE

CASHEW NUTS

CHICKEN

CHOW MEIN

CRISPY SEAWEED

GINGER

HOI SIN

KING PRAWNS

NOODLES

SATAY

SPARE RIBS

SPECIAL FRIED RICE

SPRING ROLLS

SWEET & SOUR

SZECHUAN

✱ Two or more words in a phrase, like FINDERS KEEPERS, will usually be hidden separately in the grid.

25 **KRISS KROSS**

See how quickly you can fit the listed words into the interlocking grid. The shaded squares will reveal the name of a dessert sauce.

4 LETTERS

PATH
PAWN
STAY
THEY

5 LETTERS

BOARD
INANE

6 LETTERS

ANTHEM
BRONCO
COCOON
EMBALM
ENTRAP
ICEBOX
ONLINE
VETOED

7 LETTERS

ANATOMY
SNOWMAN

8 LETTERS

ADOPTING
ENCODING
PLATINUM
WORDIEST

11 LETTERS

ACHIEVEMENT
IMPERMANENT

26 ARROWORD

The arrows show the direction in which the answer to each clue should be placed. When complete, rearrange the letters in the shaded squares to spell out a type of Tex-Mex food.

Large island off south-east Africa	▼	Opposite of "young"	▼	Stop (a criminal)	Steam bath invented in Finland	International celebrities (3,3)	▼
►				▼	▼	Experiences emotion	
Texan city		Rough first version	►			▼	
►			Regrets	►			
Air-moving device		Ms. Zellweger's first name	►				
►			Food seasoning	►			
Lowest facial bone		Warning signs	World Wide Web		Person looking after others		Cuddly bear
Scam	►	▼	▼	West __ Story, musical	▼	Bottom of a ship	▼
►				▼		▼	
Person called the same as you	►						
Cleverly contrived	Gave up work		Heroic act	►			
►							

31

ALLSPICE
ANGELICA
ANISE
ANNATTO
BASIL
BAY
BERGAMOT
BISTORT
BORAGE
BURNET
CAPER
CARAWAY
CARDAMOM
CASSIA
CAYENNE
CHERVIL

CHINESE KEYS
CINNAMON
CLARY
CLOVES
COMFREY
CORIANDER
CORKWING
COSTMARY
COSTUS
CUBEB
CUMIN SEED
CURRY
DAUN SALAM
DILL
FENNEL
FENUGREEK

GARDEN MACE
GINGER
GOLDEN NEEDLES
GRAINS of SELIM
GROUND ELDER
HEDGE GARLIC
HORSERADISH
LEMON GRASS
LOVAGE
MARJORAM
MASTIC
MEADOWSWEET
MITSUBA
MUGWORT
NUTMEG
PAPRIKA

ROSEMARY
SAFFRON
SAGE
SANDALWOOD
SANSHO
SHISO
SPEARMINT
TANSY
TARRAGON
THYME
TURMERIC
VANILLA
VERVAIN
WASABI
WOODRUFF
ZEDOARY

✱ Two or more words in a phrase, like FINDERS KEEPERS, will usually be hidden
separately in the grid.

```
T B M I T S U B E Y T C G C A S A G R G T
G E K T U N P G F A M N A D O C A R A U D
O N E G A R D E N B I O N R I R A N R A A
L N Y W H W N S A W D I L L D L K M S D U
D E E E S U F H K R A W E E C A E W Y H N
E F D I G W O R E R M G E R H R M C I M O
N G F R M M O O G G N I I S I V I O A N Y
E C E U A C B D R A N C N C N L M L M R Y
U E Z G R E C L A R Y I A T E W A S A B I
K Y R A O D E Z I E A N G G S S Z M S Y G
K E F S J L O N N D M N N M E G E N T S E
B U E U R B D O S O C A I B A S I E I N M
Z E D O A R V E W O O M K S O C X N X A T
D B E S M D L E S W S O H R L Y E K G T U
B E R G A M O T S L T N O G A R R A T E N
C O R I A N D E R A M Y R A M T S O C E R
H F B N E R E Z N D A P S L G I N G E K B
I A I Q L M O I J N R B E B U C T D D A A
E S K A D P A B O A J N R C F S L S B R S
E G S I E V A M Q S N A A D A E F T U O I
S A F F R O N O A E I D D M S P N E R B L
E R X E A P M L F C C H I C A Y E N N E A
E G V W L E A D M I L E S L H Y V R E T B
J W A A L C C P T P N E H A S E G U B A A
R L M S I H S S B S I E G R F R R B P I S
O T T A N N A I I L M Y B A O F Q V S D I
W N T B A M S N N L U H A U V M R S I C R
G Y I K V T A R R A G T N W C O A O L L E
U R T M O L E M O N W D D L A C L O Y M M
M R A R U S A N S U O S Y E K R V S Y A R
S U T S O C H C I L R A G O I E A H E C U
Y C I P S L L A M U T S O C S B T C K H T
```

In this crossword, each letter of the alphabet appears as a code number. When you have replaced the decoded numbers with their letters in the grid, fill in the boxes at the bottom to reveal a saying or phrase.

	8		18		3		18		26		13	
	12	11	22	13	25	18	5	20	19 V	12	6	15
	21		13		23		25		12 E		1	
23	25	5	1	12	16		10	13	8 R	5	18	
	8				6				21			
10	8	13	3	23	12	18	18		26	13	7	18
	12		13		8		26		1		8	
12	10	20	5		18	24	25	12	12	2	12	18
			22				19				12	
	14	12	8	17	18		12	6	3	26	4	18
	12		26		26		23		12		13	
10	12	21	26	8	13	5	20	19	12	6	15	
	9		1		17		8		18		18	

A B C D ~~E~~ F G H I J K L M N O P Q ~~R~~ S T U ~~V~~ W X Y Z

1	2	3	4	5	6	7	8 R	9	10	11	12 E	13
14	15	16	17	18	19 V	20	21	22	23	24	25	26

THE SAYING OR PHRASE IS:

20	21	20	23	16		26	23		5	22	12

21	13	17	12

FOOD FACTS

- It takes more calories to eat and digest a stick of celery than the celery contains.

- Pepperoni is the most popular pizza topping in America.

- Kiwis were once known as Chinese gooseberries.

- The first cold breakfast cereal was Shredded Wheat.

- The onion is named after a Latin word meaning "large pearl."

- The "Bell" in Taco Bell is derived from Glenn Bell, founder of the chain.

- Ears of corn always have an even number of rows.

- In 2008 Eva Longoria Parker opened a restaurant named Beso in Los Angeles. *Beso* means "kiss" in Spanish.

30 CROSSWORD

Rearrange the letters in the shaded squares to spell out a vegetable.

ACROSS

- **1** Ice-cream server (5)
- **4** Put through school (7)
- **9** Skillfully planned (8)
- **10** Stare with an open mouth (4)
- **11** Line of Cancer or Capricorn (6)
- **12** Goods transported by ship or plane (5)
- **13** Numbered musical publication (4)
- **15** Have a meal (3)
- **16** Go under (4)
- **17** Glass shape for splitting light (5)
- **19** Wildlife tour (6)
- **21** Walk with an injured leg (4)
- **22** Impose another decision upon (8)
- **23** Large sack for carrying post (7)
- **24** Strike (a door) noisily (5)

DOWN

- **2** Single seat (5)
- **3** Eight-armed creature (7)
- **5** Shop selling prepared foods (12)
- **6** Havana, cheroot, etc. (5)
- **7** Violent hurricane (7)
- **8** Cold sweet drink often served in a tall glass (3-5,4)
- **14** Red condiment made from ripe peppers (7)
- **16** Yellow food coloring (7)
- **18** Drive on (5)
- **20** Object associated with the past (5)

ANCHOVY

ASPARAGUS

CALZONE

CAPERS

DEEP-PAN

DELIVERY

GARLIC

HAM

JALAPENO

MOZZARELLA
  CHEESE

MUSHROOM

OLIVE OIL

ONION

OREGANO

PEPPERONI

PINEAPPLE

PIZZA

ROSEMARY

SPINACH

TAKEAWAY

THIN &
  CRISPY

TOMATO

TOPPING

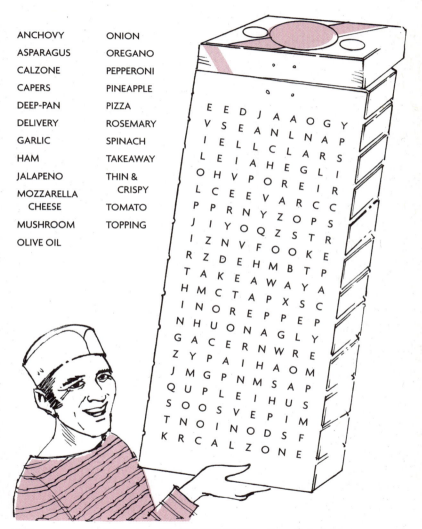

```
E E D J A A O G Y
V S E A N L N A P
I E L L C L A R S
L E I A H E G L I
O H V P O R E I R
L C E E V A R C C
P P R N Y Z O P S
J I Y O Q Z S T R
I Z N V F O O K E
R Z D E H M B T P
T A K E A W A Y A
H M C T A P X S C
I N O R E P P E P
N H U O N A G L Y
G A C E R N W R E
Z Y P A I H A O M
J M G P N M S A P
Q U P L E I H U S
S O O S V E P I M
T N O I N O D S F
K R C A L Z O N E
```

✱ Two or more words in a phrase, like FINDERS KEEPERS, will usually be hidden
  separately in the grid.

32 **KRISS KROSS**

See how quickly you can fit the listed words into the interlocking grid. The shaded squares will reveal the name of a tangy ingredient.

4 LETTERS

EPIC
LEAP
LOAN
UNIT

5 LETTERS

ATTIC
BARED
EXPEL
SALSA

6 LETTERS

ASSIGN
DARKLY
ENDEAR
EYELID
FACIAL
FILMED

7 LETTERS

COUNTER
DREAMER
FRETTED
MANACLE

8 LETTERS

LIKEABLE
MOCCASIN
REINVEST
ROTATING

13 LETTERS

GRAVITATIONAL
INEXPENSIVELY

33 ARROWORD

The arrows show the direction in which the answer to each clue should be placed. When complete, rearrange the letters in the shaded squares to spell out something to put on toast.

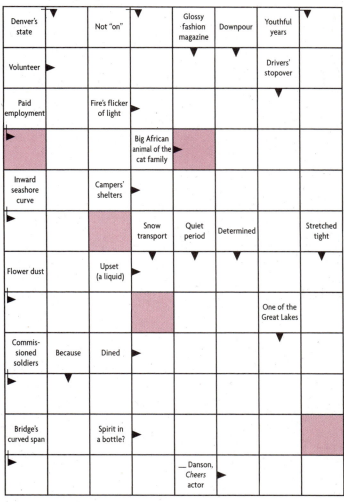

The grid clues:
- Denver's state
- Not "on"
- Glossy fashion magazine
- Downpour
- Youthful years
- Volunteer
- Drivers' stopover
- Paid employment
- Fire's flicker of light
- Big African animal of the cat family
- Inward seashore curve
- Campers' shelters
- Snow transport
- Quiet period
- Determined
- Stretched tight
- Flower dust
- Upset (a liquid)
- One of the Great Lakes
- Commissioned soldiers
- Because
- Dined
- Bridge's curved span
- Spirit in a bottle?
- ___ Danson, Cheers actor

```
        E  N  O  R  T  S  E  N  I  M  A  G  U  M  B  O
     S  E  I  K  E  E  L  A  K  C  O  C  S  O  H  U  N  C
     B  T  H  C  S  R  O  B  M  B  P  K  C  E  O  N  O  R
  T  S  O  R  R  B  I  S  Q  U  E  I  K  L  S  V  N  M  E  P
  T  U  C  U  A  B  O  U  I  L  L  A  B  A  I  S  S  E  D  O
  E  S  R  O  I  C  C  A  L  L  A  L  O  O  O  G  L  L  W  T
  E  N  E  T  T  L  C  Y  Y  I  J  Z  B  M  S  A  I  O  O  A
  M  H  E  N  L  C  L  I  O  G  Q  R  M  E  S  Z  A  G  H  G
  U  X  C  L  S  E  H  O  A  A  O  E  C  N  Y  P  T  V  C  E
  S  O  I  O  I  D  G  D  N  T  M  E  W  U  H  A  X  A  E  I
     F  T  G  C  R  R  T  H  A  E  K  U  D  C  C  O  G  H
     H  S  U  N  D  I  S  W  B  L  O  O  I  H  N  C
     B  I  A  A  A  B  N  P  N  L  R  V  O  H
     L  P  R  S  M  Y  A  E  P  A  C  S
```

AVGOLEMONO	CHOWDER	MINESTRONE	RASAM
BIRD'S-NEST	COCK-A-LEEKIE	MOCK	SANCOCHE
BISQUE	CONGEE	TURTLE	SCOTCH
BORSCHT	CONSOMME	MULLIGATAWNY	BROTH
BOUILLABAISSE	GAZPACHO	OXTAIL	SHCHI
BOUILLON	GUMBO	PEA	SKILLY
BURGOO	MADRILENE	PISTOU	STRACCIATELLA
CALLALOO	MENUDO	POTAGE	VICHYSSOISE

✱ Two or more words in a phrase, like FINDERS KEEPERS, will usually be hidden separately in the grid.

35 CODEWORD

In this crossword, each letter of the alphabet appears as a code number. When you have replaced the decoded numbers with their letters in the grid, fill in the boxes at the bottom to reveal a saying or phrase.

13	22	1	11	5	25		19	9	1	22	25	7
	5		8		16		1		13		20	
16	10	21	5		15	20	6		23	16	7	26
	18										10	
23	22	20	19	17	5		13	17	16	2	18	5
	7		1		4		16		10		7	
		13	18	22	12	5	8	1	22	7		
	7		4		1		5		5		7	
7	23	1	25	14	8		5	16	7	20	4	14
	16										5	
1	11	1	5		11	1	24 **W**		11	17	5	24
	17		22		18		5 **E**		22		3	
25	5	11	22	20	7		11 **B**	17	16	3	5	7

A B̶ C D E̶ F G H I J K L M N O P Q R S T U V W̶ X Y Z

1	2	3	4	5 **E**	6	7	8	9	10	11 **B**	12	13
14	15	16	17	18	19	20	21	22	23	24 **W**	25	26

THE SAYING OR PHRASE IS:

16	13	20	4	10	21		1	19		7	16	17	23

36 CROSSWORD

Rearrange the letters in the shaded squares to spell out a dairy product (5,6).

ACROSS

1 Salty fish often found on pizza (7)
5 Electrical discharge (5)
9 Accompaniment to food cooked outside (8,5)
10 Given a new look (8)
11 Head of the Roman Catholic Church (4)
12 Refraining from drinking alcohol (9)
16 Change place (4)
17 Film setting (8)
19 Global, worldwide (13)
21 Lift and transport (something) (5)
22 Craving water (7)

DOWN

2 Closer, more imminent (6)
3 Fit to live in (9)
4 Noisy, outspoken (5)
6 Small green vegetable (3)
7 Directions used in cooking (6)
8 Fibrous tissue attaching muscle to bone (6)
11 Black grape variety (5,4)
13 Special ability (6)
14 Front covering of the eye (6)
15 Surname of the star of *Casablanca* (6)
18 Take hold of (5)
20 Be incorrect (3)

1 What is meant by "flaking" the edges of pastry?

2 When roasting chicken, turkey, or other poultry, how do you test to see that it is cooked?

3 What is the exact metric equivalent of (a) 1 oz and (b) 1 lb?

4 Which tasty treat was considered a sin in the 17th century?

5 How do you make sure the white sets neatly around the yolk when poaching an egg?

6 What is the name of the fibers found adhering to the shells of mussels?

7 Why is it best to bake fruit tarts and similar pastry dishes in a metal pan?

8 When a dish is described as being *en brûlée*, what does it mean?

Fit the different vegetables into the grid so that the letters in the shaded column, reading down, spell out another name for the avocado.

BROCCOLI	CORN	SPINACH
CABBAGE	EGGPLANT	SPROUT
CARROT	LEEK	SWEET CORN
CAULIFLOWER	LETTUCE	TURNIP
	POTATO	

LUNCH BREAK

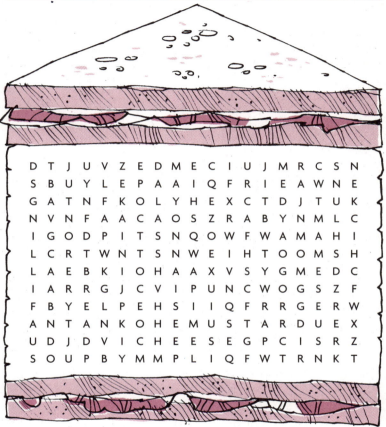

```
D  T  J  U  V  Z  E  D  M  E  C  I  U  J  M  R  C  S  N
S  B  U  Y  L  E  P  A  A  I  Q  F  R  I  E  A  W  N  E
G  A  T  N  F  K  O  L  Y  H  E  X  C  T  D  J  T  U  K
N  V  N  F  A  A  C  A  O  S  Z  R  A  B  Y  N  M  L  C
I  G  O  D  P  I  T  S  N  Q  O  W  F  W  A  M  A  H  I
L  C  R  T  W  N  T  S  N  W  E  I  H  T  O  O  M  S  H
L  A  E  B  K  I  O  H  A  A  X  V  S  Y  G  M  E  D  C
I  A  R  R  G  J  C  V  I  P  U  N  C  W  O  G  S  Z  F
F  B  Y  E  L  P  E  H  S  I  I  Q  F  R  R  G  E  R  W
A  N  T  A  N  K  O  H  E  M  U  S  T  A  R  D  U  E  X
U  D  J  D  V  I  C  H  E  E  S  E  G  P  C  I  S  R  Z
S  O  U  P  B  Y  M  M  P  L  I  Q  F  W  T  R  N  K  T
```

BREAD	HAM	SALAD
CHEESE	INSTANT SOUP	SANDWICH
CHICKEN	MAYONNAISE	SMOOTHIE
COFFEE	MICROWAVE	TEA
EGG	MINERAL WATER	TUNA
FILLING	MUSTARD	WRAP
FRUIT JUICE	PASTA	YOGURT

✱ Two or more words in a phrase, like FINDERS KEEPERS, will usually be hidden separately in the grid.

KRISS KROSS

See how quickly you can fit the listed words into the interlocking grid. The shaded squares will reveal the name of a dessert.

3 LETTERS
CUR

4 LETTERS
ALSO
DUPE
ODDS
STOP

5 LETTERS
ALIGN
CANAL
MACHO
NASAL
OFTEN
STAMP

6 LETTERS
LAPELS
NACHOS
ROCOCO
UNBORN

7 LETTERS
ANTONYM
PROVING
RINSING
SCORPIO

SWAMPED
THINNED

8 LETTERS
DISCOUNT
SPLENDID

12 LETTERS
INTOLERANTLY
PUGNACIOUSLY

41 ARROWORD

The arrows show the direction in which the answer to each clue should be placed. When complete, rearrange the letters in the shaded squares to spell out a brand of snack food.

___ Crusoe, shipwrecked man	▼	Blanket-like cloak	Frozen	Junction	Cape Town's country (5,6)	Put between (the pages)	▼
►			▼	▼	▼		
Timetable, work plan		Noise made by a dove ►				Rest sideways	
►						▼	
Playship		Put off, hinder	►				
►			Relating to the Moon	Headgear item ►			
List of available dishes	Computer message	Advance ►	▼				Disorganized
►	▼			Important test		Turn sharply	▼
Large groups of stars		Bravery ►		▼		▼	
►							
Every one of		Speed contests ►					
►			___ Poppins, Julie Andrews film ►				

42 REALLY CHEESY!

Find these cheeses from around the world.

```
H U E G Y R M B E G C R A N T C
B J S K O D E T O T O P Z I R H
A N E L I R T T Q U P U L P O E
S A A W O E G V S E R S D R F S
X S P E L G C O N E I S A A E H
F E H C Y U A Z N T C D I F U I
Y M A M C B E R N Z D I E N Q R
G R E B S L R A J E O T E B O E
J A K D L E P E H T A L Z L R A
L P I E O D H C D I T R A V A H
L Q R B P A I C A M E M B E R T
S E N W O M L A M B R O S I A V
X A B N O T L I T S E G F R H U
D Q U A R K Y Y M C R N B B J K
```

AMBROSIA	CHESHIRE	JARLSBERG
APPENZELLER	DANBO	LEICESTER
BEL PAESE	DERBY	PARMESAN
BOURSIN	EDAM	QUARK
BRIE	FETA	RACLETTE
CAERPHILLY	GORGONZOLA	ROQUEFORT
CAMEMBERT	GOUDA	STILTON
CHEDDAR	HAVARTI	TILSIT

✳ Two or more words in a phrase, like FINDERS KEEPERS, will usually be hidden
separately in the grid.

In this crossword, each letter of the alphabet appears as a code number. When you have replaced the decoded numbers with their letters in the grid, fill in the boxes at the bottom to reveal a saying or phrase.

	26	2	9	22	2	10	21	5	13	1	15	
13		8		6		2		21		13		17
8	13	10		26	25	26	6	5	21	8	24	21
1		25		20		4		25		3		8
25	16	1	5	25	26	25	9		18	6	10	24
5				1		5		5		13		23
7	21	26 **M**	26	25	24		3	25	25	10	25	5
25		21 **A**		9		4		14				13
22	21	9 **S**	12		17	21	19	25	10	8	2	1
1		22		11		8		5		6		1
25	14	21	10	2	21	1	25	9		6	24	25
24		5		13		25		21		12		8
	26	21	9	1	25	5	22	10	21	9	9	

A̶ B C D E F G H I J K L M̶ N O P Q R̶ S̶ T U V W X Y Z

1	2	3	4	5	6	7	8	9 **S**	10	11	12	13
14	15	16	17	18	19	20	21 **A**	22	23	24	25	26 **M**

THE SAYING OR PHRASE IS:

22	2	1		1	17	25		26	2	9	1	21	5	24

Using only the letters in the wordwheel, you have ten minutes to find as many words as possible, none of which may be plurals, foreign words, or proper nouns. Each word must be of three letters or more, all must contain the central letter, and letters can only be used once in every word. There is at least one nine-letter word in the wheel.

- Twelve flower designs are stamped on each side of an Oreo cookie. Each has four petals.

- Vanilla is the most popular flavor of ice cream in America.

- You're more likely to be hungry if you're cold.

- It has been traditional to serve fish with a slice of lemon since the Middle Ages, when people believed that the fruit's juice would dissolve any bones accidentally swallowed.

- Blueberry Jelly Bellies were created for Ronald Reagan.

- Peanut butter is an effective substance to remove chewing gum from hair or clothes.

- The most expensive spice in the world is saffron.

- A piece of French toast that was partially eaten by Justin Timberlake was sold on eBay.

46 **SPICE OF LIFE**

Write the answers to these clues in the grid. They are all herbs and spices. When you have finished, the letters in the shaded squares, reading down, will spell out the name of another tastebud teaser.

1 Slightly hot flavoring in the form of a tuberous root

2 Red powdered spice often used as a garnish

3 Herb in the mint family from a Mediterranean shrub

4 Leafy garnish

5 Dark brown seed pods often used to flavor desserts

6 Nail-like, brown, dried flower buds used to spice cookies and cakes

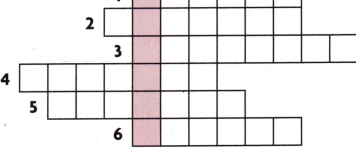

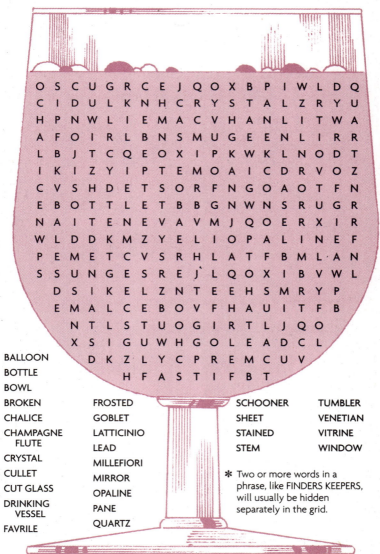

```
O S C U G R C E J Q O X B P I W L D Q
C I D U L K N H C R Y S T A L Z R Y U
H P N W L I E M A C V H A N L I T W A
A F O I R L B N S M U G E E N L I R R
L B J T C Q E O X I P K W K L N O D T
I K I Z Y I P T E M O A I C D R V O Z
C V S H D E T S O R F N G O A O T F N
E B O T T L E T B B G N W N S R U G R
N A I T E N E V A V M J Q O E R X I R
W L D D K M Z Y E L I O P A L I N E F
P E M E T C V S R H L A T F B M L A N
S S U N G E S R E J L Q O X I B V W L
D S I K E L Z N T E E H S M R Y P
E M A L C E B O V F H A U I T F B
N T L S T U O G I R T L J Q O
X S I G U W H G O L E A D C L
D K Z L Y C P R E M C U V
H F A S T I F B T
```

BALLOON
BOTTLE
BOWL
BROKEN
CHALICE
CHAMPAGNE
  FLUTE
CRYSTAL
CULLET
CUT GLASS
DRINKING
  VESSEL
FAVRILE

FROSTED
GOBLET
LATTICINIO
LEAD
MILLEFIORI
MIRROR
OPALINE
PANE
QUARTZ

SCHOONER
SHEET
STAINED
STEM

TUMBLER
VENETIAN
VITRINE
WINDOW

* Two or more words in a
phrase, like FINDERS KEEPERS,
will usually be hidden
separately in the grid.

48 KRISS KROSS

See how quickly you can fit the listed words into the interlocking grid. The shaded squares will reveal the name of a thick syrup.

3 LETTERS
FIN

4 LETTERS
CODE
ICED
REIN
USED

5 LETTERS
ADDED
ALOHA
BONGO
EXILE
MAYOR
OLIVE
RABBI
SWEET

6 LETTERS
FLAGON
VACANT

7 LETTERS
ATTEMPT
CHANCED
ORCHARD
PLEATED
SORCERY
SYNONYM

8 LETTERS
CONCERTO
GALACTIC

12 LETTERS
GRATIFYINGLY
THOUSANDFOLD

49 ARROWORD

The arrows show the direction in which the answer to each clue should be placed. When complete, rearrange the letters in the shaded squares to spell out a type of grape used to make wine.

Post-ponement	Without exception	Black and white striped animal	▼	Authentic	Occupied by private houses	Give enjoyment to	▼
▶	▼			▼	▼		
Omaha's state		Honey-maker	▶			Danny ___, Walter Mitty actor	
▶						▼	
Whiskey grain		False name	▶				
▶			Oxygen, carbon dioxide, etc.	Hair tint	▶		
State south of Minnesota	TV studio sign (2,3)	Spirited pleasure	▼				Small added photo
▶	▼			Swiss mountain range		Enthusiastic about	▼
Spears		Smooth shiny material	▶	▼		▼	
▶							
Raiders of the Lost ___ film		Sudden rush or increase	▶				
▶			Narrow hole for coins	▶			

55

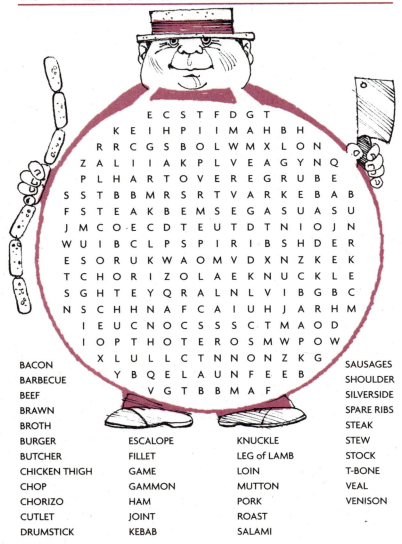

```
            E C S T F D G T
        K E I H P I I M A H B H
        R R C G S B O L W M X L O N
      Z A L I I A K P L V E A G Y N Q
      P L H A R T O V E R E G R U B E
    S S T B B M R S R T V A R K E B A B
    F S T E A K B E M S E G A S U A S U
    J M C O E C D T E U T D T N I O J N
    W U I B C L P S P I R I B S H D E R
    E S O R U K W A O M V D X N Z K E K
    T C H O R I Z O L A E K N U C K L E
    S G H T E Y Q R A L N L V I B G B C
    N S C H H N A F C A I U H J A R H M
      I E U C N O C S S S C T M A O D
      I O P T H O T E R O S M W P O W
    X L U L L C T N N O N Z K G
      Y B Q E L A U N F E E B
        V G T B B M A F
```

BACON
BARBECUE
BEEF
BRAWN
BROTH
BURGER
BUTCHER
CHICKEN THIGH
CHOP
CHORIZO
CUTLET
DRUMSTICK

ESCALOPE
FILLET
GAME
GAMMON
HAM
JOINT
KEBAB

KNUCKLE
LEG of LAMB
LOIN
MUTTON
PORK
ROAST
SALAMI

SAUSAGES
SHOULDER
SILVERSIDE
SPARE RIBS
STEAK
STEW
STOCK
T-BONE
VEAL
VENISON

* Only search for words that are in CAPITAL LETTERS. Two or more words in a phrase, like FINDERS KEEPERS, will usually be hidden separately in the grid.

Fit the pieces in the grid to spell out a a type of food flavoring in each row.

1	**R**	e	l	i	s	h
2	g	a	r	l	i	c
3	p	e	p	p	e	**R**
4	n	u	t	m	e	g
5	p	i	c	k	l	e
6	g	i	n	g	e	**R**

CROSSWORD

Rearrange the letters in the shaded squares to spell out an accompaniment to a casserole.

ACROSS

7 Speak indistinctly (4)

8 Combine (3)

9 Exhibition, show (4)

10 Stringed instrument (6)

12 Blind temporarily (6)

14 Kitchen blender (4,9)

18 Concerning Europe and North America (13)

23 ___ salad, cold dish of lettuce, anchovies, garlic, and croutons (6)

26 Feeling of extreme pleasure (6)

28 Stick together (4)

29 Young flower or leaf (3)

30 Sugar plant (4)

DOWN

1 Animal with white hair and pink eyes (6)

2 Spoken, of the mouth (4)

3 Prayer ending (4)

4 Discontinued (4)

5 Mercedes ___, car make (4)

6 ___ 13, Tom Hanks film (6)

11 Naughty child (3)

13 Plural of "is" (3)

15 Fox's lair (3)

16 Go (for) (3)

17 Male descendant (3)

19 Truly (6)

20 Large body of saltwater (3)

21 Fire remains (3)

22 Separate territory (6)

24 Trickle (4)

25 Red gemstone (4)

26 Neat (4)

27 Food grown in paddy fields (4)

53 **FOOD QUIZ**

1 What is the effect of overcooking fish (a) by conventional methods and (b) by microwave?

2 What is the meaning of the French term *mille-feuille*?

3 Which brand of beer is drunk in *The Simpsons*?

4 Crisphead, Butterhead, and Looseleaf are all varieties of what?

5 The classic version of the sauce known as pesto should contain which herb and which nuts?

6 If told to "concass" tomatoes, what should you do?

7 What type of pasta is penne?

8 What is pipérade a form of?

WORD LADDER

Change one letter at a time (but not the position of any letter) to make a new word—and move from the word at the top of the box to the word at the bottom, using the exact number of rungs provided.

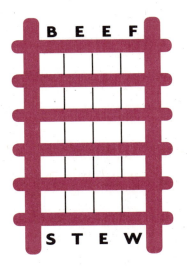

B E E F

S T E W

S	S	A	B	P	O	L	L	A	C	S
R	K	L	U	R	S	E	Z	E	M	A
E	K	I	O	A	R	H	O	J	I	S
P	C	E	P	E	T	F	R	B	X	P
P	N	D	K	J	P	E	L	I	L	V
I	I	C	G	Q	A	M	L	A	M	G
K	A	G	Y	N	O	C	I	L	N	P
M	T	T	H	P	I	C	K	I	U	S
R	U	W	H	S	E	R	T	B	H	M
L	B	U	C	Z	I	I	R	A	O	S
E	I	M	K	O	H	F	R	E	A	K
J	L	S	C	W	L	K	T	F	H	A
X	A	W	H	I	T	E	B	A	I	T
N	H	D	C	P	V	I	Y	L	L	E
H	A	K	E	H	T	Q	G	O	D	F
R	E	D	N	U	O	L	F	B	I	M
E	Y	T	O	D	R	W	R	S	U	U
W	L	R	H	R	A	B	D	T	Q	S
L	T	O	U	A	I	L	E	E	S	S
Z	E	O	S	H	N	M	K	R	R	E
P	A	J	B	C	B	S	C	F	X	L
N	I	A	D	L	O	P	R	A	W	N
P	R	K	V	I	W	I	Q	D	S	N
C	G	Y	E	P	T	R	W	A	O	H
A	N	C	H	O	V	Y	R	M	A	C
T	U	R	B	O	T	D	L	B	N	L
U	Z	S	E	O	I	A	M	K	U	A
J	S	E	C	N	S	F	X	N	T	D
P	V	A	E	I	A	G	U	L	E	B

ANCHOVY
BELUGA
CHOWDER
COD
COLEY
CRAB
EEL
FLATFISH
FLOUNDER
HAKE
HALIBUT
HERRING
KIPPER
LOBSTER
MACKEREL
MULLET
MUSSEL
PIKE
PILCHARD

PLAICE
PRAWN
RAINBOW
  TROUT
ROE
SALMON
SARDINE
SCALLOP
SEA BASS
SHARK
SHRIMP
SKATE
SKIPJACK
  TUNA
SOLE
SQUID
TURBOT
WHITEBAIT
WHITING

* Two or more words in a phrase, like FINDERS KEEPERS, will usually be hidden separately in the grid.

56 PATHFINDER

Beginning with the S in the square box, follow a continuous path to find 23 chocolate candy bars. The trail passes through each and every letter once, and may twist up, down, or sideways, but never diagonally.

S	C	K	S	Z	Y	M	P	N	Y	Z	E	R
N	I	E	R	A	S	T	H	O	Y	A	P	O
N	U	Y	A	G	N	U	O	M	D	N	K	A
C	R	C	W	Y	K	N	U	Y	A	O	W	B
H	S	K	R	O	L	D	I	T	K	A	T	A
E	E	O	Y	A	I	S	K	T	T	U	S	R
M	R	R	K	D	M	F	R	E	R	B	D	O
U	H	T	C	R	E	I	X	M	A	B	D	V
S	K	E	O	R	G	N	I	R	G	O	O	E
E	E	T	A	L	N	D	W	T	R	N	E	R
R	I	C	H	M	O	J	O	Y	Y	H	H	O
S	P	T	T	U	R	Y	B	A	B	O	O	L
T	O	O	O	T	S	I	E	R	O	L	L	S

ALMOND JOY	MR. GOODBAR	THREE MUSKETEERS
BABY RUTH	OH HENRY!	TOOTSIE ROLLS
BUTTERFINGER	PAYDAY	TOPIC
CRUNCH	ROCKY ROAD	TWIX
DOVE	ROLO	WONKA BARS
KIT KAT	SKOR	ZAGNUT
MILKY WAY	SNICKERS	ZERO
MOUNDS	SYMPHONY	

57 ARROWORD

The arrows show the direction in which the answer to each clue should be placed. When complete, rearrange the letters in the shaded squares to spell out a type of cheese.

Long Island borough ▶	Large African animal ▼	Place for posting bulletins	▼	Flying toy on a string ▼	One in charge ▼	Common joining word	▼
Style of watch		Be equal in score ▶				Grassy patch	
▶						▼	Impatient
Capital city of Italy		— of Lebanon, tree ▶					▼
▶				Female sheep ▶			
Too, as well	Popular jeans brand	Goes up in flames					
▶	▼			Demure	Mountain lion, cougar	— Baldwin, actor in The Aviator	
Countermand		Horrify ▶	▼	▼	▼		
▶							
Application		Ten-cent pieces ▶					
▶			Showerproof garments ▶				

63

BISCUIT
BLACK
BREAKFAST
BREW
CADDY

CHINA
CUP
DRINK
ELEVENSES

GREEN
KETTLE
LEAVES
MILK

MUG
POT
SAUCER
SPOON

STEAM
SUGAR
TEA-
  STRAINER
WATER

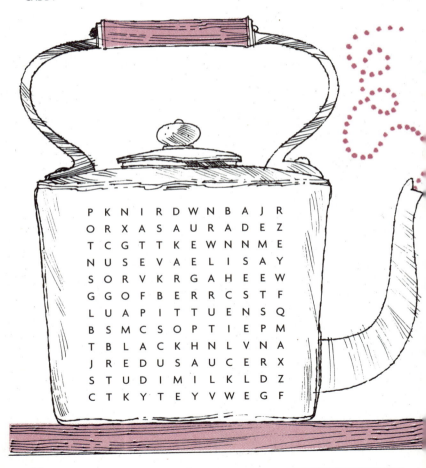

```
P  K  N  I  R  D  W  N  B  A  J  R
O  R  X  A  S  A  U  R  A  D  E  Z
T  C  G  T  T  K  E  W  N  N  M  E
N  U  S  E  V  A  E  L  I  S  A  Y
S  O  R  V  K  R  G  A  H  E  E  W
G  G  O  F  B  E  R  R  C  S  T  F
L  U  A  P  I  T  T  U  E  N  S  Q
B  S  M  C  S  O  P  T  I  E  P  M
T  B  L  A  C  K  H  N  L  V  N  A
J  R  E  D  U  S  A  U  C  E  R  X
S  T  U  D  I  M  I  L  K  L  D  Z
C  T  K  Y  T  E  Y  V  W  E  G  F
```

59 **CODEWORD**

In this crossword, each letter of the alphabet appears as a code number. When you have replaced the decoded numbers with their letters in the grid, fill in the boxes at the bottom to reveal a saying or phrase.

4	19	10	20	24		7	26	13	9	21	12	20
5		20		19		20		19		15		12
11	26	12	16	5	20	10		24	20	20	2	13
11		20		10				23				5
5	12	9	26	13	2	13		20	24	6	20	15
11		20				20		12		21		20
	21	12	20	3	3	20	18	10	5	26	24	
3		10		26		6				8		6
15	21	13	2	13		13	14	15	21	12	8	20
21				10				20		19		24
20	23 V	26 A	6 D	20		26	9	12	20	13	21	26
1		15		12		21		20		21		14
20	25	18	21	13	20	6		22	21	13	17	13

A B C ~~D~~ E F G H I J K L M N O P Q R S T U ~~V~~ W X Y Z

| 1 | 2 | 3 | 4 | 5 | 6 D | 7 | 8 | 9 | 10 | 11 | 12 | 13 |
| 14 | 15 | 16 | 17 | 18 | 19 | 20 | 21 | 22 | 23 V | 24 | 25 | 26 A |

THE SAYING OR PHRASE IS:

| 11 | 5 | 14 | | 26 | | 24 | 20 | 9 | 19 | 12 |

Using only the letters in the wordwheel, you have ten minutes to find as many words as possible, none of which may be plurals, foreign words, or proper nouns. Each word must be of three letters or more, all must contain the central letter, and letters can only be used once in every word. There is at least one nine-letter word in the wheel.

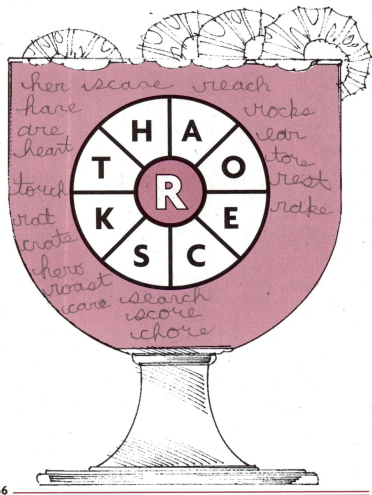

her scare reach
hare rocks
are ear
heart tore
touch rest
rat rake
crate
hero
roast
care search
score
chore

- Rice is thrown at weddings as a symbol of fertility.

- Pizza Hut was the shirt sponsor of English soccer club Fulham FC for the 2001–02 season.

- NASA approved the hot dog as a menu item on its Apollo moon flight.

- Americans spend $1 billion dining out every day.

- Pink, Beyoncé, Britney Spears, and Enrique Iglesias appeared together in a commercial for Pepsi.

- The original method of drinking sambuca was to chew two coffee beans, set the shot on fire, put it out, and drink it.

- By the time you feel thirsty, you are already dehydrated.

- From 2005 to 2007 George Clooney was the voice for Budweiser ads.

62 CROSSWORD

Rearrange the letters in the shaded squares to spell out a brand of beer.

ACROSS

- **1** Refuse to take notice of (6)
- **5** Shallow body of saltwater linked to the sea (6)
- **8** Fingers and palm (4)
- **9** Interlude (3)
- **10** Eating occasion (4)
- **11** Salt's partner (6)
- **14** Light cake (6)
- **16** Honesty (9)
- **19** Protective screen (6)
- **20** Person with a child (6)
- **21** Cold-shoulder (4)
- **23** Alcoholic drink (3)
- **25** Female horse (4)
- **26** Building material (6)
- **27** Large exotic green-skinned fruit (6)

DOWN

- **2** Small green or dark purple fruits (6)
- **3** Opposite of "young" (3)
- **4** Mayonnaise ingredient (3)
- **5** Track circuit (3)
- **6** Chewing candy (3)
- **7** Colorful citrus fruit (6)
- **12** Award or reward (5)
- **13** Sped (5)
- **14** Thick, sweet, sticky liquid (5)
- **15** External ring on a target (5)
- **17** Opportunity (6)
- **18** Desktop container for work pending (2-4)
- **22** Honey-producing insect (3)
- **23** Cart track (3)
- **24** Floor-cleaning implement (3)
- **25** Atlas entry (3)

The name of the mystery lady (three separate names) is also hidden in the puzzle.

BORN in 1977 in NEW YORK, this ACTRESS was ONLY FOUR when she was DISCOVERED by an AGENT in a RESTAURANT.

She APPEARED in MANY COMMERCIALS, and ALSO on STAGE, and FINALLY MADE a NAME for HERSELF in 1997 in the FILM *I KNOW WHAT YOU DID LAST SUMMER*.

In 2002 she STARRED as DAPHNE in *SCOOBY-DOO* AGAINST her HUSBAND, FREDDIE PRINZE JUNIOR.

Her FRIENDS CALL her SASSY. She's a BROWN BELT in TAE KWON Do, which COMES in HANDY as she PERFORMS some CHALLENGING FIGHT SCENES as the POPULAR *BUFFY, the VAMPIRE SLAYER*.

```
D H E R S E L F F C F D I D O C G S T E D
R I U I A N P S R O I E D H O F E A N G N
E O S L R R M L I M L R W M Q N H E A A A
Y T S C I R Z A E E M A M S E W I P R T B
A O K N O T L Y N S A E E C T D C V U S S
L M Z F C V S A D Y R P S L D A B J A U U
S E R A H K E N S C X P S E L E R O T O H
G E L L A R G R I T H A R A S E O R S I N
P L D H L O F A E A R F L W N D H Q E T Z
V P K R L Y L N O D G Y A C Y W H C R D F
T A F E E S P O P U L A R B R A O V I I D
M L M I N M Y S S A S R O I N U J R N M A
B A E P G N M N O W K O J D E U O A B A P
N X S B I H E U E O C G Y I A N L F D D H
B O R N N R T W S S A G E N T L H F R E N
W O N K G L E S S E R T C A Y B U F F Y E
```

* Only search for words that are in CAPITAL LETTERS. Two or more words in a phrase, like FINDERS KEEPERS, will usually be hidden separately in the grid.

64 **KRISS KROSS**

See how quickly you can fit the listed words into the interlocking grid. The shaded squares will reveal the name of a pastry ingredient.

3 LETTERS
FOR
OWN

4 LETTERS
ARCH
CUED

5 LETTERS
ADORN
ALTER
EXPAT
HORSE

6 LETTERS
ARGYLE
RUINED
SELECT
UNPLUG
UPRATE
WAGGED

7 LETTERS
PRODIGY
SUCCEED

8 LETTERS
GRADIENT
STRICTLY

9 LETTERS
AGGRIEVED
CONSIGNED
KNOWLEDGE

13 LETTERS
INEFFECTIVELY
TRANSPARENTLY

65 ARROWORD

The arrows show the direction in which the answer to each clue should be placed. When complete, rearrange the letters in the shaded squares to spell out something to drink.

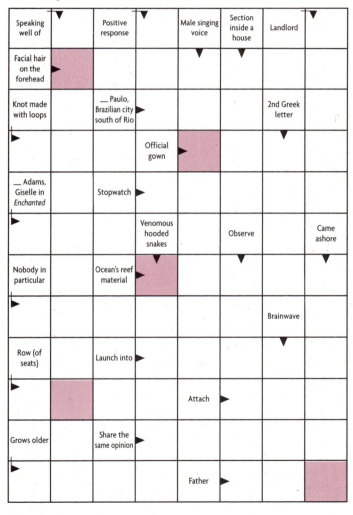

All the alimentary words are arranged in jigsaw shapes. Can you piece the puzzle together? All the letters in the grid are used. One solution is shown.

```
S  I  R  L  C  O  T  D  E  L  I  C  G  A  L  C  L  A  V  E  R
S  N  I  O  G  A  T  T  S  E  T  A  M  I  L  H  C  M  C  I  M
T  E  S  E  E  C  H  I  S  E  N  D  A  U  F  O  W  D  E  L  L
K  A  S  A  S  E  E  K  K  A  M  I  N  Y  R  S  R  E  S  H  I
W  A  O  N  E  W  A  L  A  S  A  E  N  C  O  U  S  H  P  E  C
D  L  N  I  K  O  F  R  E  N  C  R  P  A  L  E  S  I  H  E  O
O  R  G  G  O  U  S  E  R  D  H  Y  T  R  W  A  L  S  D  R  U
S  F  T  E  M  R  S  I  N  G  G  A  R  E  N  T  R  P  I  E  S
A  L  A  D  C  O  R  N  O  H  S  I  N  T  O  C  E  S  U  O  C
S  A  B  O  C  E  H  T  N  M  A  C  A  E  C  A  S  B  E  E  F
O  P  V  L  O  U  G  H  M  I  N  O  R  O  R  E  S  O  R  T  S
U  R  N  Y  U  L  S  N  A  C  H  E  E  L  E  C  R  G  A  N  O
L  E  H  C  H  H  A  M  B  U  R  E  S  E  U  Q  O  H  O  F  F
T  F  G  A  G  I  S  C  R  E  G  S  G  M  O  N  S  G  R  S  D
O  V  E  R  S  B  O  A  L  O  U  A  A  R  U  E  I  A  U  E  O
G  G  E  D  E  L  I  E  I  R  C  E  M  M  O  N  E  M  V  R  E
```

BEEF STROGANOFF	COLESLAW	DINNER PARTY	~~MACARONI CHEESE~~
BOILED EGG	CORN ON THE COB	ENTRECOTE	SAUCE
CALORIE	COTTAGE CHEESE	FRENCH DRESSING	SEASONING
CASSEROLE	COUSCOUS	GALLIMAUFRY	SHEPHERD'S PIE
CLAM CHOWDER	CROQUE MONSIEUR	GAME	SIRLOIN STEAK
	DELICATESSEN	GAMMON	SUSHI
		GARNISH	TIKKA MASALA
		GOURMET	VERMICELLI
		HAGGIS	WALDORF SALAD
		HAMBURGER	WOK
		HORS D'OEUVRE	
		LEFTOVERS	

67 CODEWORD

In this crossword, each letter of the alphabet appears as a code number. When you have replaced the decoded numbers with their letters in the grid, fill in the boxes at the bottom to reveal a saying or phrase.

	12	13	25	7	4	3	19		7	6	6	22
7		23 N		14		25		22		5		5
17	5	4 T		24	11	9	5	16	24	4	7	11
7		25 I		22		7		26		4		24
16	1	7	24	18		22	16	13	3	3	22	
4				7				18		7		10
7	8	6	24	26	15		26	13	11	11	7	26
11		25		24				3				25
	8	5	26	4	24	3		5	2	4	7	23
22		3		25		25		13		1		15
18	26	5	18	5	13	23	11	22		5	10	3
13		20		23		7		3		22		7
26	24	19	22		7	23	21	19	8	7	22	

A B C D E F G H~~I~~ J K L M~~N~~ O P Q R S~~T~~ U V W X Y Z

1	2	3	4 T	5	6	7	8	9	10	11	12	13
14	15	16	17	18	19	20	21	22	23 N	24	25 I	26

THE SAYING OR PHRASE IS:

13	18	22	7	4		4	1	7

24	18	18	3	7	16	24	26	4

68 CROSSWORD

Rearrange the letters in the shaded squares to spell out a fruit.

ACROSS

1 Mountain range in which Banff and Jasper are located (7)
5 Complicated swindle (4)
10 Make error-free (5)
11 Feathers on a bird (7)
12 Popular white meat (7)
14 Square block (4)
16 Pay back (money) (6)
18 Two-way music system (6)
20 Set of two (4)
21 Give a new look to (7)
24 Fundamental (7)
25 Huge person (5)
27 Vehicle's gas container (4)
28 Knot-shaped snack (7)

DOWN

2 Be in the red (3)
3 Brand-name camera and film company (5)
4 Increase in size or importance (6)
6 Sauce accompaniment for roast turkey (9)
7 Congregate (4)
8 Cosmetic for darkening the eyelashes (7)
9 Sweet white wine (6)
13 Rising costs and prices (9)
15 Neediness (7)
17 Usual, regular (6)
19 Fervent request (6)
22 Vision (5)
23 Notice (4)
26 Tailless monkey (3)

1 What kind of steak would you use for Steak Diane?

2 When making a fruit tart with pastry below and above the fruit, what ingredients could you use to "mop up" the fruit juice and so help to prevent the bottom pastry from becoming soggy?

3 Why were tomatoes once known as love apples?

4 What is Popeye's favorite food?

5 Which dessert was named after a Russian ballerina?

6 What is the difference between nutmeg and mace?

7 What is the name given to egg white?

8 What was the origin of mincemeat?

HIDDEN WORDS

Fifteen things associated with dining, food, and drink (including the example PEAR) are hidden among the letters of this passage. How many can you spot?

You know, I never get u**p ear**ly, and if I have time, a lie-in is a treat! If I go to sleep late, I won't get up before the afternoon. Sleep, or kip as I call it, isn't unalloyed pleasure, though—half is horrible, thanks to nightmares! I once saw a terrible vision at night that would provoke universal torment. It's something which I personally hope can be effectively avoided in the future: I dreamed of my reflection in the mirror, first thing in the morning!!!

```
L  R  C  M  E  O  S  S  B  G  D  A  H  W
A  U  P  A  E  N  A  H  N  E  B  R  T  H
G  E  E  S  L  K  G  I  E  S  E  H  U  I
E  U  R  C  E  V  L  A  I  R  C  R  O  S
R  Q  R  H  E  K  A  N  P  T  R  P  M  K
R  I  Y  N  R  A  T  D  O  M  O  Y  R  Y
E  L  I  A  T  H  I  C  O  R  A  O  E  N
T  W  P  P  E  I  S  N  T  S  E  H  V  A
T  S  L  P  T  I  V  A  U  Q  A  D  C  L
I  T  H  S  T  E  Q  U  I  L  A  I  I  N
B  U  R  G  U  N  D  Y  T  E  R  A  L  C
S  I  T  S  A  P  B  R  A  N  D  Y  G  S
```

Today we are going to the liquor store.
The remaining letters spell out a fitting message.

ABSINTHE	CALVADOS	PASTIS	SHERRY
AQUAVIT	CHAMPAGNE	PERRY	SPARKLING
BEER	CIDER	PORT	TEQUILA
BITTER	CLARET	SAKE	VERMOUTH
BRANDY	LAGER	SCHNAPPS	WHISKY
BURGUNDY	LIQUEUR	SCOTCH	WINE

See how quickly you can fit the listed words into the interlocking grid. The shaded squares will reveal the name of a stew.

4 LETTERS

ACID
DUTY
WILY
YELL

5 LETTERS

ATTIC
EJECT
IDEAL
OCEAN
OVOID
UNCAP

6 LETTERS

AERIAL
ALLURE
EXODUS
GIRDER

NUDISM
SHIRTS

7 LETTERS

ASSURED
CHEATED
CRUDITE
INSPECT
OIL WELL
SETTLED
SLAYING
WAIVING

12 LETTERS

FELICITOUSLY
VOLUPTUOUSLY

73 **ARROWORD**

The arrows show the direction in which the answer to each clue should be placed. When complete, rearrange the letters in the shaded squares to spell out a type of sauce dip.

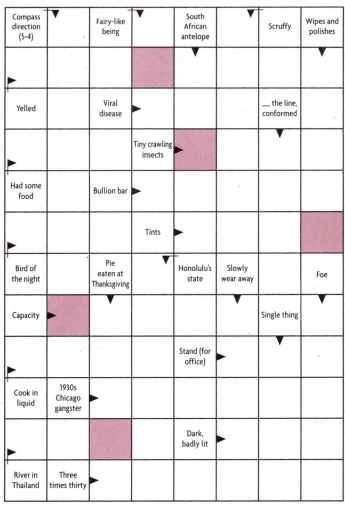

Compass direction (5-4)	▼	Fairy-like being	▼	South African antelope	▼	Scruffy	Wipes and polishes
▶				▼			▼
Yelled		Viral disease	▶			__ the line, conformed	
▶		Tiny crawling insects	▶			▼	
Had some food		Bullion bar	▶				
▶			Tints	▶			
Bird of the night		Pie eaten at Thanksgiving	▼	Honolulu's state	Slowly wear away		Foe
Capacity	▶	▼			▼	Single thing	▼
▶				Stand (for office)	▶	▼	
Cook in liquid	1930s Chicago gangster	▶					
▶				Dark, badly lit	▶		
River in Thailand	Three times thirty	▶					

The words are arranged in spirals, starting or finishing at the center, clockwise or counterclockwise. Some of the spirals may overlap. One solution is shown.

BARTENDER
BEVERAGES
BOTTLETOP
CHAMPAGNE
CHERRYADE
COCKTAILS
COINTREAU
CORKSCREW
CREAM SODA
DRY SHERRY
GINGER ALE
HALF A PINT

HERBAL TEA
HOT COFFEE
LIME JUICE
MILKSHAKE
MOONSHINE
ORANGEADE
~~RHINE WINE~~
RYE WHISKY
SODA WATER
SOFT DRINK
TAWNY PORT
WINEGLASS

H	E	D	A	Q	I	O	R	A	M	X
O	H	C	Y	K	U	D	E	N	G	P
T	E	R	R	Y	S	A	E	G	J	A
V	E	N	I	D	H	E	R	B	E	V
R	O	M	H	C	E	A	B	E	S	E
W	O	N	S	Z	T	L	A	G	A	R
E	F	N	L	B	D	R	Y	H	Q	I
M	X	C	O	C	R	Y	S	O	K	U
G	P	L	S	K	R	E	H	S	O	F
T	Y	I	A	T	S	S	A	N	K	T
S	J	A	R	H	I	W	L	I	R	D
U	A	E	N	E	N	E	G	V	D	R
O	C	R	I	W	E	C	C	O	R	W
I	N	T	Z	E	F	N	E	W	K	L
B	H	Q	I	E	E	F	R	C	S	M
C	H	A	X	O	H	F	O	K	U	G
N	E	M	P	T	C	O	T	Y	K	S
G	A	P	Y	S	J	A	V	Y	R	I
D	R	C	W	Z	A	D	O	E	W	H
E	G	I	N	F	R	C	S	T	R	O
N	L	E	G	L	E	A	M	A	T	P
B	A	R	E	T	H	Q	I	W	N	Y
M	X	O	S	A	L	I	M	O	K	U
G	P	D	A	W	C	E	E	T	N	I
R	E	D	T	Y	I	U	J	A	H	P
A	B	N	E	K	A	S	J	L	F	A
R	T	E	I	M	H	A	P	O	T	V
D	R	C	L	K	S	W	O	B	E	Z
E	F	N	L	B	H	Q	T	T	L	I

In this crossword, each letter of the alphabet appears as a code number. When you have replaced the decoded numbers with their letters in the grid, fill in the boxes at the bottom to reveal a saying or phrase.

5	21	6	14	11	6		21	1	17	11	11	1
21		25		9		16		20		10		2
6	11	2	12	21	15	11		15	19	19	6	25
25		7		13		15		20		1		24
	24	10	21	11		4	11	6	11	11	24	14
24		11				6		19				11
20	26	6	18	11	15		24	10	19	6	11	15
1				23		13				3		6
25	20	4	10	11	20	21		14	20	21	10	
2		20		24		8		21 U		20		19
16	2	6	2	25		8	19	25 T	25	10	11	13
11		2		19		22		24 C		19		13
6	21	26	13	15	22		24	14	19	15	21	6

A B C̶ D E F G H I J K L M N O P Q R S T̶ U̶ V W X Y Z

| 1 | 2 | 3 | 4 | 5 | 6 | 7 | 8 | 9 | 10 | 11 | 12 | 13 |
| 14 | 15 | 16 | 17 | 18 | 19 | 20 | 21 U | 22 | 23 | 24 C | 25 T | 26 |

THE SAYING OR PHRASE IS:

| 16 | 20 | 15 | 2 | 11 | 25 | 22 | | 2 | 6 | | 25 | 14 | 11 |

| 6 | 1 | 2 | 24 | 11 | | 19 | 7 | | 10 | 2 | 7 | 11 |

Beginning with the P in the square box, follow a continuous path to find 12 songs. The trail passes through each and every letter once, and may twist up, down, or sideways, but never diagonally.

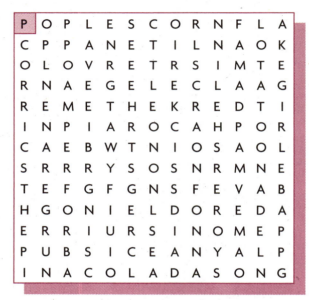

P	O	P	L	E	S	C	O	R	N	F	L	A
C	P	P	A	N	E	T	I	L	N	A	O	K
O	L	O	V	R	E	T	R	S	I	M	T	E
R	N	A	E	G	E	L	E	C	L	A	A	G
R	E	M	E	T	H	E	K	R	E	D	T	I
I	N	P	I	A	R	O	C	A	H	P	O	R
C	A	E	B	W	T	N	I	O	S	A	O	L
S	R	R	R	Y	S	O	S	N	R	M	N	E
T	E	F	G	F	G	N	S	F	E	V	A	B
H	G	O	N	I	E	L	D	O	R	E	D	A
E	R	R	I	U	R	S	I	N	O	M	E	P
P	U	B	S	I	C	E	A	N	Y	A	L	P
I	N	A	C	O	L	A	D	A	S	O	N	G

AMERICAN PIE

ANIMAL CRACKERS

CORNFLAKE GIRL

CRUISING FOR BURGERS

LITTLE GREEN APPLES

MASHED POTATO

MAYONNAISE

ONE BAD APPLE

POPCORN LOVE

STRAWBERRY FIELDS
FOREVER

THE ONION SONG

THE PINA COLADA SONG

- The character Fonzie in *Happy Days* has a fear of liver.

- Jennifer Aniston's favorite cuisine is Mexican.

- British sailors were called Limeys because they were given lime juice to help prevent them from getting scurvy.

- Raspberries used to be called hind berries.

- Frank Carney founded Pizza Hut in 1958.

- Rum is filtered through charcoal to get its light color.

- Over 10,000 varieties of wine grapes exist in the world.

- October is National Pizza Month in America.

Rearrange the letters in the shaded squares to spell out a flavor of ice cream.

ACROSS

7 Less straight (of hair) (7)
9 Bake in the oven (5)
10 Water formed by condensation at night (3)
11 Inspired, encouraged (9)
12 Very important (5)
14 Downpour (7)
16 Arctic reindeer (7)
18 Underlying foundation (5)
19 Melbourne's country (9)
20 Disney's medical dwarf (3)
21 Sweet corn (5)
22 Infinite (7)

DOWN

1 Scholarly or theoretical (8)
2 Sketch (4)
3 Cook gently (6)
4 One guiding a vehicle (6)
5 Restaurant employee (8)
6 Collar fastener (4)
8 French vegetable casserole (11)
13 ___ *Park*, Steven Spielberg dinosaur film (8)
15 Lawsuit setting a precedent (4,4)
17 Grain used in malt liquor (6)
18 Spirit distilled from wine (6)
19 Group of soldiers (4)
20 Restrict your food intake (4)

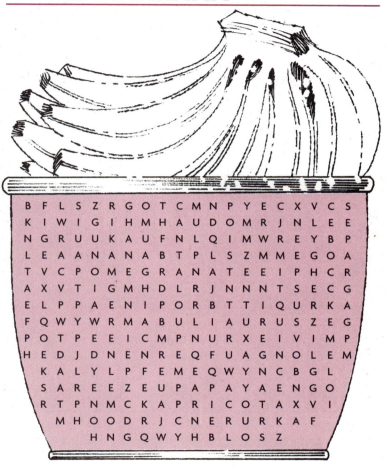

```
B F L S Z R G O T C M N P Y E C X V C S
K I W I G I H M H A U D O M R J N L E E
N G R U U K A U F N L Q I M W R E Y B P
L E A A N A N A B T P L S Z M M E G O A
T V C P O M E G R A N A T E E I P H C R
A X V T I G M H D L R J N N N T S E C G
E L P P A E N I P O R B T T I Q U R K A
F Q W Y W R M A B U L I A U R U S Z E G
P O T P E E I C M P N U R X E I V I M P
H E D J D N E N R E Q F U A G N O L E M
  K A L Y L P F E M E Q W Y N C B G L
  S A R E E Z E U P A P A Y A E N G O
  R T P N M C K A P R I C O T A X V I
  M H O O D R J C N E R U R K A F
  H N G Q W Y H B L O S Z
```

APRICOT	GRAPEFRUIT	LEMON	ORANGE	PLUM
BANANA	GRAPES	LIME	PAPAYA	POME-GRANATE
CANTALOUPE	GUAVA	MANGO	PEACH	QUINCE
CHERRY	HONEYDEW	MEDLAR	PEAR	RHUBARB
CLEMENTINE	KIWI	MELON	PERSIMMON	TANGERINE
FIG	KUMQUAT	NECTARINE	PINEAPPLE	

In this crossword, each letter of the alphabet appears as a code number. When you have replaced the decoded numbers with their letters in the grid, fill in the boxes at the bottom to reveal a saying or phrase.

2		14		19				9		19		9
19 **P**	8 **A**	22 **Y**	14	20	11	19		8	13	2	21	3
20		5		8		8		11		5		15
11	5	19	20	22		21	3	20	3	8	14	3
17		4				8		6				20
4	12	12		8	4	4	8	11	7	3	26	
14		5		5		21		21		20		19
	8	14	4	3	21	12	11	26		3	23	3
10				7		12				25		21
2	7	24	20	8	14	19		19	3	8	24	16
11		11		6		3		8		4		8
3	18	4	12	20		21	3	1	21	12	2	19
4		3		3				3		21		14

A B C D E F G H I J K L M N O ~~P~~ Q R S T U V W X ~~Y~~ Z

| 1 | 2 | 3 | 4 | 5 | 6 | 7 | 8 **A** | 9 | 10 | 11 | 12 | 13 |
| 14 | 15 | 16 | 17 | 18 | 19 **P** | 20 | 21 | 22 **Y** | 23 | 24 | 25 | 26 |

THE SAYING OR PHRASE IS:

| 8 | 19 | 11 | 3 | 24 | 3 | | 12 | 17 | | 24 | 8 | 23 | 3 |

81 ARROWORD

The arrows show the direction in which the answer to each clue should be placed. When complete, rearrange the letters in the shaded squares to spell out something to eat for breakfast.

Mexico's money unit	Of the same value	Lounge serving spirits (8,3)	▼	Letters from admirers (3,4)	▼	Makes believe	▼
►	▼			Atmosphere ►			
Donald __, cartoon character		Swindle ►				Skin complaint	
►				Small carpet	►	▼	
Entreaty		Follow step by step ►					
►				Holiday __, Bing Crosby film ►			
__ out, scoop water from a boat	Defendant's whereabouts claim	Sat at the stoplight ►					
►	▼			Copied	Group of three people	Put your name to	
Leonardo __, actor		Small flying mammals ►		▼	▼	▼	Single number
►							▼
Youngster		Rule over a country ►					
►			Finished ►				

```
Z A Q U A N D O N G O
N L I C B S F W K I H
G L B M M I A V H H I
Q I W D A L T C O Q C
T U P I N D A T U X K
L Q G U T T A E E W O
E O T R S U E C E R R
U C R I O N N H A Y Y
A J P Z S U S O N M C
S F K L G A N B C M V
H Q A W C D O D T O P
I N X L E R E K N O C
D T R E B L I F U U A
G N A W A R R U B C T
R Y A N B R J Z E N U
C S F A U E K R G B R
A M V C T M A H Q W G
D C B E T E L O T P U
I X O P E D L E U R R
Y A J R R O Z N C S G
F C H I N C A P I N S
H K T P U O G T B A B
M A I U T C U V O H R
Q N Z W N N D U O T A
E P I E T A A X L E Z
U R Y S L R E A C J I
Z N E C I N S P O F L
K H G B M V U H L Q W
C A L M O N D T A D O
```

ACORN	COQUILLA
ALMOND	FILBERT
ARECA	GROUNDNUT
BETEL	GRUGRU
BITTER	HAZELNUT
BRAZIL	HICKORY
BURRAWANG	MACADAMIA
BUTTERNUT	PEANUT
CASHEW	PECAN
CHESTNUT	PINE
CHINCAPIN	PISTACHIO
COCO-DE-MER	QUANDONG
COCONUT	QUEENSLAND
COLA	SAOUARI
CONKER	WALNUT

83 STAIRCASE

Place these seven soup-related items in the horizontal rows so that the letters in the diagonal staircase spell out the name of another item relating to soup.

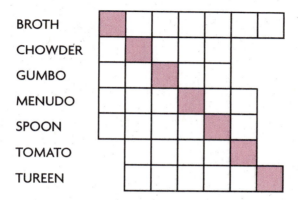

BROTH

CHOWDER

GUMBO

MENUDO

SPOON

TOMATO

TUREEN

Rearrange the letters in the shaded squares to spell out a Tex-Mex dish (5,3,5).

ACROSS

7 Open-textured Italian bread (8)
8 Boundary mark (4)
9 Small marine creature (6)
10 Divine messenger (5)
11 Firmly against (4)
12 Strips of vegetable or fruit skin (8)
14 German spirit (8)
18 Singlet (4)
20 Measuring stick (5)
22 Factory produce (6)
23 Wine-bottle stopper (4)
24 Reduce in size (8)

DOWN

1 Enclosed or surrounded by (6)
2 Nothingness (8)
3 Increase in intensity (4,2)
4 Cocktail delicacy (6)
5 Banner, pennant (4)
6 Switch off (6)
13 Requesting (8)
15 Bugs Bunny's vegetable (6)
16 Carnival procession (6)
17 Wet and gusty (6)
19 Gourd-like vegetable (6)
21 Large pool of freshwater (4)

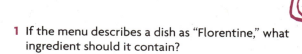

85 FOOD QUIZ

1 If the menu describes a dish as "Florentine," what ingredient should it contain?

2 When frying fish, how do you ensure that the batter or egg and bread-crumb coating adheres to the fish?

3 What is another name for the alligator pear?

4 What important nutrient do eggs provide?

5 What are lamingtons?

6 How do the fresh sardines we buy differ from those in cans?

7 What is the most expensive spice in the world?

8 How does James Bond take his martini?

86 SIX-PACK

Fit the six listed fruits into the pattern of adjoining hexagons, using one letter per triangle, and forming all words clockwise. Adjoining triangles of adjacent hexagons always have the same letter as each other. We've put in a starter letter to get you going.

CITRON

DAMSON

LOQUAT

MEDLAR

PAPAYA

QUINCE

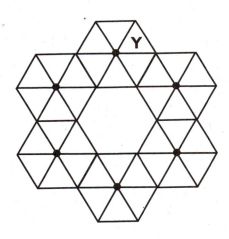

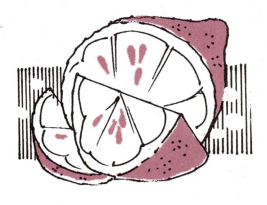

```
        T I Y R G G Y
      B O B R N U Y A T A S
    C M R R O A E S E E H C U
  E A S E O C L P A R S L E Y W
S T T B O A W W O R C E S T E R C
O O N T M T T N L G V E R D E Y H
P O A U O E E S I A D N A L L O H A M
A R V L R H R M E F B L E J S E E S O
C T E E W S E G S P E D I S X D R S R
E U C E B R A B I M A Q L K E A A E N
C A R B O N A R A A R W O Z D L T U A
T B V I R G Y H N N N H I R S U R R Y
L E C E U O C S N W A I A A K O A T Y
  I R L L E C P O O I T V E A M T V
  V L I B O H S Y M S E T B R E A D
    F I Y J U E A U E C T D X R Q
    K H A Z T M B H B N I G R
      G C K Y E U A N I C U
        S I P W T T M
```

AIOLI
BARBECUE
BEARNAISE
BECHAMEL
BOLOGNESE
BREAD
BROWN
CARBONARA
CHASSEUR
CHEESE

CHILI
CRANBERRY
GRAVY
GUACAMOLE
HOLLANDAISE
KETCHUP
MAYONNAISE
MINT

MORNAY
MUSTARD
PARSLEY
PESTO
REMOULADE
SALSA VERDE
SATAY
SOY

SWEET
and SOUR
TABASCO
TARTARE
TERIYAKI
TOMATO
VELOUTE
VINAIGRETTE
WHITE
WORCESTER

✳ Only search for words that are in CAPITAL LETTERS. Two or more words in a phrase, like FINDERS KEEPERS, will usually be hidden separately in the grid.

88 **KRISS KROSS**

See how quickly you can fit the listed words into the interlocking grid. The shaded squares will reveal the name of a cake topping.

4 LETTERS
FEAR
RAMP
STAY
WIPE

5 LETTERS
ANVIL
DEIGN
DIARY
IDLED
LIVER
OCCUR
RACES
WIRED

7 LETTERS
ASSUAGE
CULPRIT
FESTIVE
INSULIN
MARTINI
PERSONA
PROVISO
TERRAIN

9 LETTERS
PRECISION

10 LETTERS
ANNOYINGLY
CONFORMIST

13 LETTERS
RECRIMINATORY

Change one letter at a time (but not the position of any letter) to make a new word—and move from the word at the top of the box to the word at the bottom, using the exact number of rungs provided.

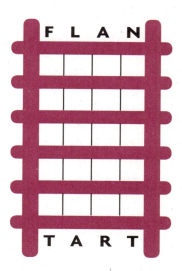

F L A N

T A R T

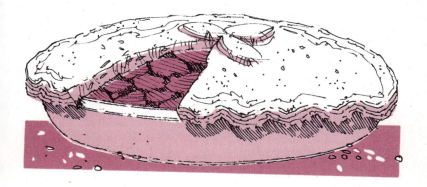

```
N F L N I K P M U P K C P P U E X L
C R T E S W U D C J C A N M E Q V E
A C O L T C A H H U Z I O Y W A B E
R A R C I T A T C I C E B E R G S K
R B G S T R U U E B I B A R L H O K
O B P M D E M C F R B E E T H U P T
T A K O O B E R E O C C O P U E X P
C G T O E N A W T C A R G I S D I Y
J E A R T D I A S C I A E N W N O R
M Q V H I E M O L O R H D S S S T E
S W I S S O K Z N L E A I R S O A L
Y W H U T B R C I I L G A F K C T E
P U E M X T S C O A E P D J A N O C
H C A N I P S M S R C T U R N I P Q
```

BEET	CELERY	LETTUCE	PUMPKIN	SWISS CHARD
BROCCOLI	CUCUMBER	MUSHROOM	RADISH	TOMATO
CABBAGE	GARLIC	ONION	ROCKET	TURNIP
CAPSICUM	ICEBERG	PARSNIP	SALAD	WATERCRESS
CARROT	KOHLRABI	PEAS	SPINACH	
CELERIAC	LEEK	POTATO	SWEET CORN	

✶ Two or more words in a phrase, like FINDERS KEEPERS, will usually be hidden
separately in the grid.

CODEWORD

In this crossword, each letter of the alphabet appears as a code number. When you have replaced the decoded numbers with their letters in the grid, fill in the boxes at the bottom to reveal a saying or phrase.

15		10		2				8		6		9
17	7	18	25	11	26	10		18	9	26	15	26
19		7		10		18		7		7		19
23	18	10	26	15		9	26	15	10	18	8	15
12		16				19		3				10
19	20	20		19	15	17	7	16	9 **B**	26 **E**	15 **S**	
20		20		4		17		5		1		5
	7	19	4	26	23	18	11	15		19	16	20
15				7		23				21		19
10	16	21	5	19	23	16		12	18	5	26	24
11		19		14		15		7		20		5
22	20	11	13	26		10	7	19	5	26	6	26
22		20		15				9		15		23

A B C D E F G H I J K L M N O P Q R S T U V W X Y Z

| 1 | 2 | 3 | 4 | 5 | 6 | 7 | 8 | 9 **B** | 10 | 11 | 12 | 13 |
| 14 | 15 **S** | 16 | 17 | 18 | 19 | 20 | 21 | 22 | 23 | 24 | 25 | 26 **E** |

THE SAYING OR PHRASE IS:

| 12 | 18 | 23 | , | 10 | 5 | 11 | 10 | 19 | 20 | 20 | 24 | 18 | 11 | 7 |

| 26 | 14 | 14 | 15 | 16 | 23 | 18 | 23 | 26 | 9 | 19 | 15 | 13 | 26 | 10 |

Here's a quotation from Woody Allen on the dangers of dieting. The words have dropped out of position into the columns below. Can you restore the quote?

		LOSE			WE
	BE			TWENTY	
POUNDS		.	WE		
		POUNDS			
GENIUS,		,		LOVE	
.					

~~POUNDS~~	~~BE~~	~~POUNDS~~	~~WE~~	MAY	AND
~~GENIUS~~	THE	HAVE	THE	~~TWENTY~~	~~WE~~
MAY	WE	HUMANITY	TWENTY	POUNDS	BE
LOSING	OUR	LOSING	THAT	CONTAIN	OUR
HONESTY	WE	~~LOSE~~	OUR	~~LOVE~~	BEST
WHEN					

- Another name for cranberries is bounce berries.

- Mel Blanc, who played the voice of Bugs Bunny, was allergic to carrots.

- Beaujolais Nouveau is only released on the third Thursday of every November.

- Cosmopolitans are the preferred cocktails of the characters in *Sex and the City*.

- The longest barbecue ever took place in Jamaica, lasting over seven months.

- George Clooney had a keg of Guinness installed in his dressing room when he filmed *Oceans 11*.

- Each year in Oaxaca, Mexico, Night of the Radishes takes place on December 23. Carved radishes depict scenes of the Christmas celebration.

- Under U.S. government regulations 90 percent of peanut butter has to be peanuts.

94 CROSSWORD

Rearrange the letters in the shaded squares to spell out a type of salad dressing.

ACROSS

7 Dark, milk syrup (8)

8 Steep decline (4)

9 Spanish dish with rice, seafood, chicken, etc. (6)

10 Painter (6)

11 High-protein pulses (7)

13 Villain (5)

15 Dangerous (5)

17 Hungarian stew of beef, vegetables, and paprika (7)

19 United (6)

21 Large South American bird (6)

23 Passport endorsement (4)

24 One of the main components of a Martini cocktail (8)

DOWN

1 State east of Nebraska (4)

2 Classical form of dance (6)

3 As a rule (7)

4 Earth's largest continent (4)

5 Chief journalist on a newspaper (6)

6 N. African semolina granules (8)

12 Relating to a series of events (8)

14 Snack made from roasted grain (7)

16 U.S. "Sunflower State" (6)

18 England's capital city (6)

20 Plunge head first (into water) (4)

22 Sworn declaration to tell the truth in court (4)

Al DENTE
BOLOGNESE
CARBONARA
FARFALLE
FETTUCCINE
FORK
FUSILLI
GARLIC
GNOCCHI
LADLE
LASAGNE
LINGUINE
MACARONI
NOODLES
OLIVE OIL
PARMESAN CHEESE

PASTA
PENNE
PESTO
RADIATORE
RAVIOLI
RIGATONI
SAUCE
SHELLS
SPAGHETTI
SPOON
TAGLIATELLI
TOMATO
TORTELLINI
VERMICELLI
VONGOLE

```
T E I H C C O N G I H
M O N F A R F A L L E
A Y R I V J G L Q L S
C I U T C O E N P I E
A F A D E C N L E S N
R L R E I L U G O U N
O W I M N T L T O F E
N C R N V G S I T L P
I E O X G E A B N E E
V K T Z P U M S H I F
J G A D Q S I I A U N
P F G A E D L N E L N
B O L O G N E S E A S
E V I L O C T R S C P
W T A C H V O E A T O
X B T E K K M R I O O
Z M E H Y R B L J M N
G S L Q A O O S I A U
E N L P N I P F F T A
D L I A V N E R W O T
C V R A I O O X B K Z
M A R H T T Y J G Q S
I E R O T A I D A R N
S A U C E G T U N O P
F A D L H I E S O R L
W T C V G R O D A A I
C I L R A G L X D P O
B K Z M P E H L Y J G
Q S I U S H E L L S N
```

✳ Two or more words in a phrase, like FINDERS KEEPERS, will usually be hidden separately in the grid.

KRISS KROSS

See how quickly you can fit the listed words into the interlocking grid. The shaded squares will reveal the name of a broth.

3 LETTERS

EAT
ELF

4 LETTERS

EDGE
FRET
HEED
SAPS

5 LETTERS

ELUDE
PHOTO
ROSTI
TASTY

6 LETTERS

MEADOW
RADIUS
STEAMY
WEB CAM

7 LETTERS

DEMONIC
DYNAMIC
STRATUM
YOUNGER

8 LETTERS

ASSENTED
COIFFURE
HUSTINGS
SUN VISOR

9 LETTERS

ALLOCATED
SPIRALLED

11 LETTERS

MELODICALLY

The arrows show the direction in which the answer to each clue should be placed. When complete, rearrange the letters in the shaded squares to spell out something to put on a burger.

Christian __, fashion designer	▼	Place where crops are grown	▼	Julia __, Runaway Bride star	▼	Picture houses ▼
Rocky Mountain state ►						Division of geological time
Movie launch	Sense organ of balance		__ Stiller, Meet the Parents star ►		▼	
►		▼				
Part of a sentence	Herb often used on pizzas		Finish level	Symbol of Aries ►		
►	▼		▼	Take a breath		Increase in length
From Austin or Dallas		Gets out of bed ►		▼		▼
►					Country bordering Iraq	Takes food
Foot of an animal		Pale ►			▼	▼
►			Precinct ►			
Male child		Put (seeds) into the ground ►				
►			Concludes ►			

BUTTERSCOTCH

CHOCOLATE

CONE

CREAM

DAIRY

FLAKE

FLAVOR

FUDGE

MELTING

PISTACHIO

RASPBERRY

RUM and RAISIN

SAUCE

SCOOP

SOFT

SPOON

STICK

STRAWBERRY

TOFFEE

TOPPING

VANILLA

WAFFLE

WHIPPED

```
P O O C S L U V N B T R Q S
M Y Z K S L A V S U K F A W
X Z R T A N D V P T M U O F
M I I R I Q S E Q T C S L S
G C O L E F L A K E F P C J
K Y L Y T B L J J R Z O N O
Q A I H A K W A U S A O G F
W A F F L E N A V C E N O C
T V F P O G V B R O I G S W
Q V E D C I Y D N T R O Y T
A P O E O J B T L C S R C H
U W W H G H E O H A A I
E Y N C X M S T F K M B
P I S T A C H I O F A R
H O G E U M U G Y S E C
G N I P P O T R T X R E
P A D Z T D R E B X C D
C N R S F E R G G I M Y
L W A X B P H B M D R C
P K I P Y P F J W I U X
I R S B Y I U Z A M R F
C A I Z L H V D R U J D
R Q N K E W H P O R T L
```

✱ Only search for words that are
in CAPITAL LETTERS. Two or
more words in a phrase, like
FINDERS KEEPERS, will usually be
hidden separately in the grid.

99 CODEWORD

In this crossword, each letter of the alphabet appears as a code number. When you have replaced the decoded numbers with their letters in the grid, fill in the boxes at the bottom to reveal a saying or phrase.

	19	23	9	9	23	8	4		16	9	25	19 **G**
5		8		26		6		16		7		26 **A**
26	21	7	1	22		7	14	23	19	1	26	9 **M**
18				22		26		15		23		7
12	7	16	22	7	1	3		15	26	3	18	
26		14				16		6		19		1
6	25	25	4	7	2		2	7	24	20	16	7
4		1		11		26				7		26
	16	22	25	14		8	1	7	26	16	7	2
23		16		7		23		17				23
22	20	9	13	6	7	2		20	3	22	23	6
8		7		16		23		23		25		18
10	26	3	4		16	8	7	14	22	1	7	

A B C·D E F G H I J K L M N O P Q R S T U V W X Y Z

| 1 | 2 | 3 | 4 | 5· | 6 | 7 | 8 | 9 **M** | 10 | 11 | 12 | 13 |
| 14 | 15 | 16 | 17 | 18 | 19 **G** | 20 | 21 | 22 | 23 | 24 | 25 | 26 **A** |

THE SAYING OR PHRASE IS:

| | 22 | 10 | 7 | | 13 | 7 | 16 | 22 | | 22 | 10 | 23 | 3 | 19 | |
| 16 | 23 | 3 | 8 | 7 | | 16 | 6 | 23 | 8 | 7 | 2 | | 13 | 1 | 7 | 26 | 2 |

Rearrange the letters in the shaded squares to spell out a type of fast food.

ACROSS

6 Hard, hairy seed of the palm tree (7)
7 Creature in *Jaws* (5)
9 Pleasure excursion (4)
10 Green or purple vegetable (8)
11 Cooked in a pot (6)
13 Length of film (4)
15 Somehow sense (4)
16 Metal pin for piercing meat (6)
18 Outline of a course of studies (8)
21 True to life (4)
22 Privileged group (5)
23 Flat pieces of Italian pasta (7)

DOWN

1 Company directors (5)
2 Medical institution (8)
3 Speechless (4)
4 Smart, fashionable (4)
5 Luggage cart (7)
8 Swiss cheese dip (6)
12 Pungent Japanese condiment, like horseradish (6)
13 Loaf often used with pastrami (3,5)
14 Use (waste materials) again (7)
17 Holy person (5)
19 Opposite of "early" (4)
20 Mark of a wound (4)

1 "Have it your way" is the slogan of which food chain?

2 Charqui, pronounced "sharkey" in Spanish is another name for what?

3 If advised to place a baked custard in a "bain-marie" while baking, what must you do?

4 What is a favorite coating for fresh herrings in Scotland?

5 For what purpose is a mandoline used?

6 What is the classic French name for a savory egg flan?

7 One of America's famous cakes is known as an angel food cake. What makes it so light?

8 What is the main ingredient of soy sauce?

Each word in a clue can be preceded by the same two letters to make three new words. The three pairs of letters will then spell out a vegetable.

1 KEY, LICE, TENT

2 BOO, LENT, ROT

3 DAY, TALLY, WARD

```
E  P  S  N  L  Q  U  G  Z  H  K  M  O  A  G  P
M  A  D  R  O  A  N  S  K  C  O  R  F  R  A  G
O  S  E  H  C  I  W  D  N  A  S  S  E  R  N  H
C  D  Z  P  L  N  T  N  U  M  K  E  T  I  J  A
L  E  I  G  R  V  X  C  M  O  T  Y  T  E  F  T
E  S  N  W  E  I  L  I  U  I  C  E  G  N  S  S
W  I  E  G  B  T  P  W  N  D  E  S  U  Y  E  S
M  V  D  B  M  A  M  G  A  M  O  T  E  E  G  A
J  Y  R  B  U  T  L  E  R  I  V  R  S  K  X  C
H  G  A  K  C  I  W  B  I  N  T  L  T  R  A  Y
T  W  G  T  U  O  C  A  N  A  P  E  S  N  Q  C
S  N  H  R  C  N  T  E  F  F  U  B  R  M  I  F
```

BUFFET

BUTLER

CAKES

CANAPES

CUCUMBER SANDWICHES

FROCKS

GARDEN PARTY

GREETING

GUESTS

HATS

HOSTESS

INTRODUCTION

INVITATION

LAWN

MEETING

MINGLING

TRAY

WAITER

WELCOME

✱ Two or more words in a phrase, like FINDERS KEEPERS, will usually be hidden separately in the grid.

See how quickly you can fit the listed words into the interlocking grid. The shaded squares will reveal a hidden word.

3 LETTERS

EAU
FEN
ION
NIT
SIN

4 LETTERS

AURA
DAMS
KINK
LIPS
PLAN
TURF
UGLY
VILE

5 LETTERS

FAULT
INEPT
JUROR
SLANT

6 LETTERS

BANKED
BONSAI
BUSILY
ELDEST
GEMINI
INFANT
SOWING
WAVING

9 LETTERS

INTENSITY
VILIFYING

105 **ARROWORD**

The arrows show the direction in which the answer to each clue should be placed. When complete, rearrange the letters in the shaded squares to spell out a brand of cereal.

	▼		▼				▼
Baggage-reclaim conveyor		Volcanic outpouring		Roof space	Reads letter by letter	Glenn __, *Damages* star	
►					▼		
Soft part of a bed		Number of years in a decade		Showered, poured		Bottom of a shoe	
►		▼		▼		▼	
Tin __, *Wizard of Oz* character	Ordinary		__ vera, health juice ►				
►	▼		Poorly, unwell				Film's final two words? (3,3)
Powerful aircraft		Com-mencement ►					▼
►			Small particle of matter		Brand of sandwich cookie	Street	
Two-wheeled vehicle		Love intensely	▼		▼	▼	
►				Eggs of fish ►			
Set of players		Atlantic or Pacific, e.g. ►					
►				Not even ►			

111

All are welcome!

ALFRESCO	CORN on the COB	LAWN	SAUSAGES
APRON	CUTLERY	LOTS of SALAD	SKEWER
BARBECUE	DRUMSTICKS	MARINADE	SMOKE
BEER	FISH	MEAT	SOFT DRINKS
BOWLS	FOLDING CHAIRS	NEIGHBORS	SOOT
BRING a BOTTLE	FRIENDS	ONIONS	SPARE RIBS
BURGERS	GARDEN	PARTY	STEAKS
BURNING	GLASSES	PATIO	SUMMER
CARVING	GRILL	PLATES	TABLE
CHARCOAL	GUESTS	PORK CHOPS	TOMATOES
CHEF	HUSBAND	POTATOES	TRAY
CHICKEN WINGS	INVITATION	PUDDINGS	VEGETARIAN
CHILDREN	KETCHUP	RICE	WIFE
CONSERVATORY	KITCHEN	SAUCE	WINE
COOKING OIL			

✱ Only search for words that are in CAPITAL LETTERS. Two or more words in a phrase, like FINDERS KEEPERS, will usually be hidden separately in the grid.

```
R M M D P O R K U L S T E C O R N E C C B
S I R G V D N E U I K D O B O E R R N A F
O A P U B E O I N O A T Z M R V I Z R I S
O Q U E O T G V O N E J M D A A C B W C W
C H E S A B I E I N T U L H H T E C U A S
G R U T A T H R T P S I H C G C O A O W L
M N O S A G A G U A H D U R U P S E O R G
A P I T B M E D I C R R S E R A P S S N R
R W I N N A D O C E J I B L D R G R I L L
I O S D R I N K S O N N A T P T R K I L N
N L M E N U T A G V N J N U O Y O R N T W
A S O G K F B E N E C S D C H O G L I A A
D I K T O O K T I G H I E O C T S P R B L
M D L S S E M S D E A F S R E G R U B L S
S A U S A G E S D T R C A R V I N A C L B
A L F R E S C O U A C S E O T A T O P O P
X A T R H B G C P R O C G M F G T C C A C
W S B S I U N H I I A B A N A E U O T R H
N P I S E E I I C A L L U R I T T I R P E
I F R S K E N L O N A P D R L W O A V Y F
K I T C H E N D N S G K U E G N I D L O F
O W I C S M F R S K N F R H I E R N C P G
O H T B E H R E E C I Y I O C E R K H N N
C I C A S X P B R I V N N T M T C I I S E
K Z Y H S L A O V T R A A M A I E R L P I
N E D R A G X W A S A E U B T P B K D O G
A M T T L I I L T M C S L S K E W E R H H
T P E S G F R Q O U P Y M T S O L T E C B
R S R M E B L S R R O U H C T E K A W O O
G Y E O T A M O T D R A L T T O B B W R R
Y A R T N T A E M D B N I N R U B L A E S
S O I T A T I V N I F R I E N N S E L I R
```

In this crossword, each letter of the alphabet appears as a code number. When you have replaced the decoded numbers with their letters in the grid, fill in the boxes at the bottom to reveal a saying or phrase.

18		24		2				10		8		12
8	20	13	2 **T**	4 **O**	17 **R**		9	23	13	1	8	3
17		3		17		3		12		18		1
4	23	2	3	2	12	26	8	20		4	5	8
13		8		4		22						22
1	12	22	20	13	20	12	2	8		4	20	20
		8		3		19		7		6		
15	8	20		8	24	4	25	8	14	8	22	2
17						19		17		17		17
4	17	16		15	17	23	13	2	1	12	21	8
11		4		23		8		13		1		22
8	10	23	13	22	8		23	22	13	2	8	20
22		2		21				19		3		3

A B C D E F G H I J K L M N Ø P Q Ж S Ж U V W X Y Z

1	2 **T**	3	4 **O**	5	6	7	8	9	10	11	12	13
14	15	16	17 **R**	18	19	20	21	22	23	24	25	26

THE SAYING OR PHRASE IS:

13	22	12		22	23	2	3	18	8	24	24

- Dr Pepper is said to be named in honor of Dr. Charles T. Pepper, a drugstore owner who concocted the drink. A clerk at his store, Wade Morrison, reproduced the drink and called it Dr Pepper.

- Meat pie is considered the Australian national dish.

- Brad Pitt appeared in a Heineken commercial. It was shown in 25 different countries but only once in America (during the 2005 Super Bowl).

- In Indonesia deep-fried monkey toes are eaten off the bone.

- Quote from Miss Piggy: "After all the trouble you go to, you get about as much actual 'food' out of eating an artichoke as you would from licking 30 or 40 postage stamps."

- Each year from March 1–9, Eurochocolate takes place in Italy. At this event the streets are filled with vendors selling nothing but chocolate.

- On average there are 75 grapes to each cluster.

- When rearranged, the letters in "whiskey" spell "key wish," and those in "moonshine" spell "in no homes."

Beginning with the C in the square box, follow a continuous path to find 17 cereals. The trail passes through each and every letter once, and may twist up, down, or sideways, but never diagonally.

C	E	S	C	O	A	K	E	S	F	K	Y	C
A	I	I	R	R	L	A	I	O	R	C	U	H
P	P	S	K	N	F	L	C	O	O	O	L	A
N	C	H	A	O	C	K	E	T	L	P	S	R
C	N	Q	O	C	R	U	P	S	S	A	C	M
R	U	U	T	S	F	I	T	Y	A	R	U	S
P	S	I	I	B	A	R	S	P	T	I	Z	A
A	L	P	H	A	I	O	P	E	B	B	S	P
E	N	N	A	M	S	P	N	C	S	L	E	P
Y	O	H	T	A	I	N	R	O	K	C	A	L
S	M	V	I	K	N	B	R	I	S	P	J	E
C	A	G	N	I	A	R	C	F	I	L	E	A
K	S	G	O	L	D	E	N	E	C	E	R	L

ALPHA-BITS

APPLE JACKS

CAP'N CRUNCH

COCOA KRISPIES

CORN FLAKES

CORN POPS

FROOT LOOPS

FRUITY PEBBLES

GOLDEN CRISP

HONEY SMACKS

KING VITAMAN

LIFE CEREAL

LUCKY CHARMS

QUISP

RAISIN BRAN

SPECIAL K

ZUCARITAS

110 WATERMELON WORDS

All these words are made from the letters in WATERMELON.

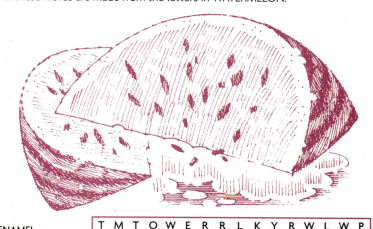

ENAMEL	T M T O W E R R L K Y R W L W P
ENROL	R L N E W E L E O L X O E A H E
ETERNAL	A A R L N M F N E G M M R N Q I
LAMENT	M E U E A M Z T A A A M O D W W
LEMON	B R W N N N O A N N C S T E W O
TEA	R A L M O M R L E E T A N R O T
MATRON	L E E R E L J E T R O W E L O T
MENTOR	V L M K Y T A P T E T O M L X H
MERLOT	E A O O R M R T F E N Q R G I M
METEOR	L U N Z T A D O B R E E W N L O
METRO	T C S J V E T L K O M E T E O R
MOLTEN	N O R T A M Y P O N A A W X H A
MORALE	E R W M F L O R N E L O E G Q L
MOTEL	I U Z N A D W B N T T C S T J E

NEWEL	OWNER	RENEWAL	TENOR	TOWN	WARM
NORMAL	REALM	RENTAL	TOWEL	TRAM	WET
ORNATE	REMOTE	TALON	TOWER	TROWEL	WOMAN

✱ Two or more words in a phrase, like FINDERS KEEPERS, will usually be hidden separately in the grid.

111 **WORDWHEEL**

Using only the letters in the wordwheel, you have ten minutes to find as many words as possible, none of which may be plurals, foreign words, or proper nouns. Each word must be of three letters or more, all must contain the central letter, and letters can only be used once in every word. There is at least one nine-letter word in the wheel.

The arrows show the direction in which the answer to each clue should be placed. When complete, rearrange the letters in the shaded squares to spell out a brand of beer.

	▼		▼	Asian exercise philosophy	Bought and sold	Sultan's wives	▼
Blocking vote		(They) used to be					
►				Typically English drink ►	▼		
State bordering Maryland		Piece of wood		Tusked seal-like creature		Assess the value of	
►		· ▼		▼		▼	
Joke	Sale inviting bids		__ and Eve, Bible's first people ►				
►	▼		Rent out (accommodation) ►				Staggered giddily
High playing card		Military command ►					▼
►			Open, spacious		Knowledge (abr.)	Herb often used when cooking fish	
Very short skirt		Separately ►	▼		▼	▼	
►				Nothing ►			
Exclusively		Long firearm ►					
►				Elderly	►		

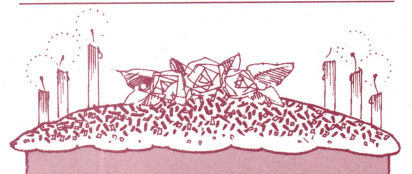

```
B  Y  G  N  I  D  D  E  W  C  W  B  J  L  Y  K  T  C
T  V  A  L  E  N  T  I  N  E  S  R  O  A  I  N  H  C
H  E  Z  D  O  T  E  O  L  L  F  S  G  J  E  R  O  W
V  O  S  H  H  D  I  C  N  E  U  M  P  M  I  N  C  Q
D  X  U  T  B  T  O  J  L  B  Y  K  E  S  T  O  C  R
A  R  I  S  O  M  R  C  Z  R  O  R  T  P  N  I  A  T
E  E  I  M  E  P  F  I  S  A  I  E  G  E  E  T  S  W
V  M  O  V  A  W  H  D  B  T  N  N  G  C  M  A  I  U
M  R  O  S  I  P  A  Q  E  I  X  B  R  I  E  U  O  J
P  L  S  H  Y  N  K  R  N  O  R  A  I  A  G  D  N  I
R  E  T  S  A  E  G  G  M  N  C  Z  V  L  A  A  O  T
D  E  Y  R  A  S  R  E  V  I  N  N  A  F  G  R  S  W
C  H  R  I  S  T  M  A  S  G  N  W  M  V  N  G  E  H
S  E  N  D  O  F  F  D  N  U  M  G  L  P  E  N  Q  X
```

ANNIVERSARY	ENGAGEMENT	RETIREMENT
BIRTHDAY	GRADUATION	SEND-OFF
CELEBRATION	HOUSE-WARMING	SPECIAL OCCASION
CHRISTENING	NEW JOB	VALENTINE'S
CHRISTMAS	PASSED the DRIVING TEST	WEDDING
EASTER	PROMOTION	WELCOME HOME

✱ Only search for words that are in CAPITAL LETTERS. Two or more words in a phrase, like FINDERS KEEPERS, will usually be hidden separately in the grid.

In this crossword, each letter of the alphabet appears as a code number. When you have replaced the decoded numbers with their letters in the grid, fill in the boxes at the bottom to reveal a saying or phrase.

11		16		7		6		7		19		4
15	26	4	22	20	11	8	10	6		21	6	22
26		22		11		20		26		3		9
3	16	9	17	16	5	26		20	11	3	11	17
11						2				5		6
9	11	18		24	11	6	7	16	20	11	8	
22		26		16				11		9		22
	6	9	16	25	12	26	5	5		3	11	3
16		13				4						16
3	26	21	23	22 E		11	9	22	14	26	8	7
5		22		9 N		26		7		4		11
22	26	7		4 V	16	20	26	8	11	16	21	6
6		6		1		1		24		25		15

A B C D ~~E~~ F G H I J K L M ~~N~~ O P Q R S T U ~~V~~ W X Y Z

1	2	3	4 V	5	6	7	8	9 N	10	11	12	13
14	15	16	17	18	19	20	21	22 E	23	24	25	26

THE SAYING OR PHRASE IS:

21	6	22		1	16	21	20		5	16	26	12

115 CROSSWORD

Rearrange the letters in the shaded squares to spell out a wine-growing state of the United States.

ACROSS

1 James Bond's preferred cocktail (7)
5 Main ingredient of bouillabaisse (4)
8 Travelers' accommodation (5)
9 Partially coincide (7)
11 Fill (a suitcase) (4)
12 System of letters (8)
15 Bee's produce (5)
16 Tough cotton material used for jeans (5)
19 Hard brown tree fruit, roasted and eaten (8)
21 Front of the lower jaw (4)
23 Person making a new home (7)
25 Stadium (5)
26 Front of the head (4)
27 Put air into (7)

DOWN

2 Vegetable that occurs in globe and Jerusalem varieties (9)
3 Wall covering (4)
4 Piece of ribbon-shaped pasta (6)
5 Name given to several coniferous trees (3)
6 Unnerve (5)
7 Buys things (5)
10 Repeated (sound) (6)
13 Sunniest (9)
14 Concerned with hiring goods (6)
17 Move faster than (6)
18 Work (flour) into dough (5)
20 "Laughing" animal (5)
22 Drop down (4)
24 Stand for a golf ball (3)

1 What is the difference between orange rind and orange zest?

2 What is meant by the term *beurre manié*?

3 What is the name of raw granular brown sugar?

4 Poire Belle Hélène is a famous dessert. With what kind of sauce is it served?

5 What is the oldest known vegetable to man?

6 What is the most popular way of serving eggs?

7 When you buy cooked crab, how do you judge that it is full of flesh and is not watery?

8 What kind of oil is best when making mayonnaise or salad dressings?

117 **DRINKS CABINET**

Can you fit the ten jigsaw pieces in the grid so that the name of an alcoholic drink appears down each of the seven columns?

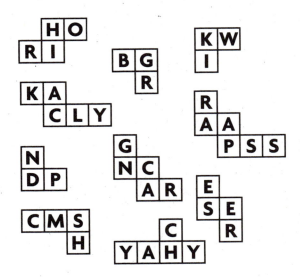

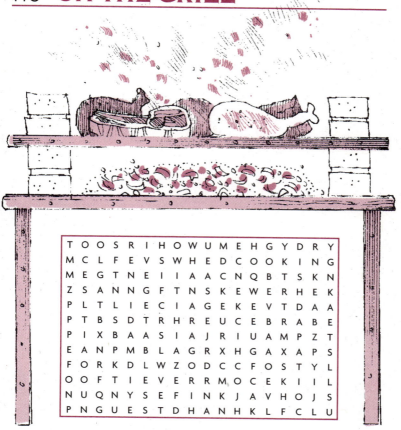

```
T  O  O  S  R  I  H  O  W  U  M  E  H  G  Y  D  R  Y
M  C  L  F  E  V  S  W  H  E  D  C  O  O  K  I  N  G
M  E  G  T  N  E  I  I  A  A  C  N  Q  B  T  S  K  N
Z  S  A  N  N  G  F  T  N  S  K  E  W  E  R  H  E  K
P  L  T  L  I  E  C  I  A  G  E  K  E  V  T  D  A  A
P  T  B  S  D  T  R  H  R  E  U  C  E  B  R  A  B  E
P  I  X  B  A  A  S  I  A  J  R  I  U  A  M  P  Z  T
E  A  N  P  M  B  L  A  G  R  X  H  G  A  X  A  P  S
F  O  R  K  D  L  W  Z  O  D  C  C  F  O  S  T  Y  L
O  O  F  T  I  E  V  E  R  R  M  O  C  E  K  I  I  L
N  U  Q  N  Y  S  E  F  I  N  K  J  A  V  H  O  J  S
P  N  G  U  E  S  T  D  H  A  N  H  K  L  F  C  L  U
```

APRON	DISH	HOT	PLATE
BARBECUE	FISH	KNIFE	ROASTING
CHARCOAL	FOIL	MARINADE	SAUCE
CHEF	FORK	MEAL	SKEWER
CHICKEN	GARDEN	MEAT	SOOT
COOKING	GRILLING	PARTY	STEAK
DINNER	GUEST	PATIO	VEGETABLES

119 **KRISS KROSS**

See how quickly you can fit the listed words into the interlocking grid. The shaded squares will reveal hidden vegetables.

4 LETTERS

DATA
SPEW
USED
WADE

5 LETTERS

ELFIN
INAPT
MINER
MINUS

NYLON
POKER

6 LETTERS

ABATED
EDITED
EVENLY
NODDED
SCRIBE
STODGY

7 LETTERS

BEADING
EDDYING
EYESORE
PREMISE
REBUKED
REFUSED
STABLED
TABULAR

11 LETTERS

DISTRIBUTOR
INESTIMABLY

The arrows show the direction in which the answer to each clue should be placed. When complete, rearrange the letters in the shaded squares to spell out a fruit used to make a sauce.

Classical female dancer		___ Now or Never, Elvis hit		Month before May	Food dressing	Manage with what you have (4,2)	
Animated Disney classic		Health resort				Give for a while	
			Guideline to be obeyed				
Scheming		Cut into cubes					
			Jay ___, U.S. talk-show host				
Be in tears		Stupid person		Outline of a meeting	Agreement to stop fighting		Brushed (the floor)
Saturday ___ Fever, film						Author unknown	
				Not cooked			
Green semi-precious stone	Harmonized (with) (2,4)						
				Police officer			
Small forest	Natural ability						

```
            A U F P F N L F Y
          H J R Y G I C J I Z K B O
        D A O W I N E L N S X C K I M
      T M H E T V I Q G L O G I A L U T
      B A T T E R R E P F I N T L R R Y
    C U S T A R D R         C N S J E Z B R
    D W I E L S L             X G A K M O T
    H V Q O O I                 T G A D U P
    G F N L C                     R N Y C J
    S N Z K O                     E H O L E
    B W I D H W                   V I E S X Y
    K N E C C M T               D H V Q O R G
    G A U E I Y P F           N O L R Y A C J
    S U O I T P M U R C S Z U B D G W I E
      S X K M T T U H V Q O G G U A U P
      Y M M U Y A F U N L R H S Y C D J
        Z B D W S I E R S X N K M O T
          H V Q T O G A T U U P O F
            N Y L R Y C S T G
```

BATTER

CHOCOLATE

CUSTARD

DOUGHNUT

FILLING

FINGER-LICKING
  GOOD

HOLE

HOT OIL

ICING

JAM

RING

SCRUMPTIOUS

STICKY

SUGARY

SWEET

TASTY

TREAT

VENDOR

YUMMY

✳ Two or more words in a phrase, like FINDERS KEEPERS, will usually be hidden separately in the grid.

122 CODEWORD

In this crossword, each letter of the alphabet appears as a code number. When you have replaced the decoded numbers with their letters in the grid, fill in the boxes at the bottom to reveal a saying or phrase.

18		2		18 **P**		25		25		6		22
22	18	26	13	23 **H**		26	4	3	2	7	4	8
22		3		26 **O**		19		26		4		16
3	26	19	6	11	3	22		11	6	8	21	26
2		22		4		17		22				20
	14	8	19	6	17	8	4	2	23	22	16	
		10								8		
	22	2	2	22	8	10	4	6	3	3	1	
12				4		23		13		6		6
6	16	26	18	10		22	24	10	26	17	10	2
3		18		23		15		14		25		4
2	9	14	22	22	5	22		6	23	22	6	16
22		2		17		2		3		16		22

A B C D E F G H I J K L M N O P Q R S T U V W X Y Z

1	2	3	4	5	6	7	8	9	10	11	12	13
14	15	16	17	18 **P**	19	20	21	22	23 **H**	24	25	26 **O**

THE SAYING OR PHRASE IS:

22	6	10		23	14	15	11	3	22		18	4	22

WORD LADDER

Change one letter at a time (but not the position of any letter) to make a new word—and move from the word at the top of the box to the word at the bottom, using the exact number of rungs provided.

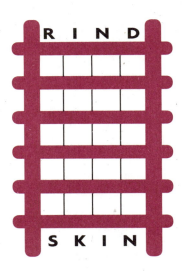

R I N D

S K I N

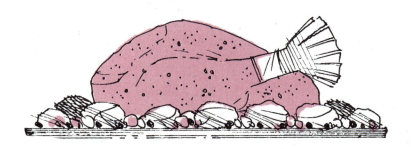

- Pizza Fest is held every year in September. People come together in Naples, Italy, to celebrate its most famous export.

- Jennifer Lopez owns a restaurant called Madres. *Madres* means "mothers" in Spanish.

- White wine should be served chilled, whereas red wine should be served just below room temperature.

- Before mercury, brandy was used in thermometers.

- Ajiato is a chicken soup from Colombia.

- Feminist poet Carol Ann Duffy uses the onion as a metaphor of love and relationships in her poem "Valentine."

- Among Polynesians, the banana was traditionally a taboo food for women.

- The pumpkin is a fruit, not a vegetable.

125 CROSSWORD

Rearrange the letters in the shaded squares to spell out a breakfast food (5,4).

ACROSS

1 On numerous occasions (5)
4 Brushed with the lips (6)
10 Outdoor venue for musicians (9)
11 Female sheep (3)
12 U.S. "Pine Tree State" (5)
13 Nonessential (6)
14 Splendid in appearance (11)
18 Red salad food (6)
20 Notion of perfection (5)
23 Paid sportsperson (3)
24 Plum variety (9)
25 Sounded the same (6)
26 Old and New Testaments (5)

DOWN

2 Mushroom-like plants (5)
3 From China or Japan, perhaps (7)
5 Book's alphabetical list (5)
6 Administer an official oath to (5,2)
7 Animal possessing antlers (4)
8 44th president of the U.S.A. (5)
9 Variety of cabbage with edible white buds (11)
15 Word of regret (7)
16 Italian red wine produced in the region of Tuscany (7)
17 Extraterrestrial (5)
19 Corner (5)
21 Communicate over the Web (5)
22 Goad (4)

M	S	E	K	A	L	H	J	E	K	U
S	O	I	D	L	A	V	I	V	Y	S
E	Y	Z	S	L	A	N	A	C	P	R
V	N	I	Z	B	N	X	S	A	A	I
O	A	W	Q	A	C	A	G	A	R	V
R	C	I	N	D	R	H	P	A	T	E
G	S	M	T	A	E	E	V	L	M	R
Z	U	E	O	T	C	I	L	O	E	S
R	T	D	T	M	O	I	R	L	G	S
A	N	I	V	L	P	R	T	T	A	L
F	R	T	I	H	L	J	A	A	E	K
U	Y	E	S	E	E	H	C	V	V	I
I	B	R	P	X	A	S	O	W	A	A
Q	T	R	C	O	N	L	A	D	I	P
Z	O	A	E	N	I	H	S	N	U	S
R	T	N	L	V	N	M	I	G	N	P
V	U	E	E	Y	G	D	T	P	A	E
L	R	A	P	A	R	M	E	S	A	N
F	I	N	Z	A	L	E	T	H	J	I
E	N	Z	S	F	L	A	W	K	U	W
Y	I	I	B	E	A	X	S	O	W	Q
P	C	A	D	C	B	S	Z	O	T	E
C	H	I	A	N	T	I	H	R	C	N
A	L	P	S	E	O	M	G	I	A	N
P	V	P	T	R	O	L	N	I	O	F
H	I	J	E	O	F	E	L	K	U	N
Y	I	S	B	L	V	A	X	S	W	Q
C	A	D	A	F	T	M	I	L	A	N
Z	S	I	C	I	L	Y	O	R	M	G

ALPS
ART
CANALS
CHIANTI
FASHION
FLORENCE
FOOTBALL
ITALIAN
ITALY
LAKES
LEANING TOWER
   of PISA
MEDITERRANEAN
MILAN
MOZZARELLA
NAPLES
OLIVE GROVES
OPERA
PARMESAN
   CHEESE
PASTA
PAVAROTTI
PIZZA
RAVIOLI
RIVERS
ROME
SARDINIA
SICILY
SPAGHETTI
SUNSHINE
TURIN
TUSCANY
VATICAN
VENICE
VIVALDI
WINE

✳ Only search for words that are in CAPITAL LETTERS. Two or more words in a
   phrase, like FINDERS KEEPERS, will usually be hidden separately in the grid.

127 **PATHFINDER**

Beginning with the B in the square box, follow a continuous path to find 14 films with a food theme. The trail passes through each and every letter once, and may twist up, down, or sideways, but never diagonally.

B	A	N	M	Y	I	C	A	T	L	U	B	B
A	N	A	S	S	T	P	Z	H	C	T	S	R
M	A	H	E	A	T	I	Z	E	B	F	A	E
B	U	L	L	T	A	R	N	A	R	K	K	A
G	R	I	U	O	E	A	D	M	E	A	F	A
E	I	L	L	B	R	H	T	P	U	O	T	S
R	H	U	S	R	E	E	U	C	K	S	A	T
G	T	N	O	C	G	G	D	Y	N	A	F	T
R	E	S	H	O	N	I	L	S	A	Y	F	I
I	L	L	C	L	H	I	L	S	L	E	R	C
D	E	I	R	A	R	A	G	U	P	U	O	A
G	E	N	F	T	T	O	T	O	I	L	S	K
R	E	T	O	M	A	E	S	R	T	L	A	E

BANANAS

BREAKFAST AT TIFFANY'S

THE BREAKFAST CLUB

CHOCOLAT

DUCK SOUP

FRIED GREEN TOMATOES

THE GINGERBREAD MAN

HAMBURGER HILL

LAYER CAKE

MYSTIC PIZZA

RATATOUILLE

SUGARHILL

SUNSET GRILL

TORTILLA SOUP

128 ARROWORD

The arrows show the direction in which the answer to each clue should be placed. When complete, rearrange the letters in the shaded squares to spell out a way of serving eggs.

Boxers' exercise equipment	▼	Salty oriental sauce	▼	Scarcely any	Worship	Rise gradually	▼
Good for nothing ►	▼			▼			
The present ►			Large wild ox		Acclaim		
►			Christian __, Batman Begins star	▼		▼	
Glacial		Italian fashion city	►				
►			Collar fastener	►			
Receding tide		Something worth having	Emotional		Spicy Mexican sauce or dip		Soft French cap
Grassed areas	►	▼	▼		▼	Baked, broad or runner?	▼
►				President Lincoln's nickname	►	▼	
More, in addition	Shopkeeper ►						
►			Container for return mail (inits) ►				
Extending far down	Oppressive leader ►						

135

BARBECUE CHICKEN
BEAN CURD
CHILI
COCONUT MILK
CORIANDER
FISH CURRY
FRIED RICE with PINEAPPLE
GINGER
LEMONGRASS
MANGO
MORNING GLORY
NOODLES
OYSTER SAUCE
PRAWNS with GARLIC
SWEET and SOUR
   MEATBALLS
TOM YAM GUNG
WATER SPINACH

T	E	E	W	S	O	P	S	R	G	E	C	D	I
O	Y	S	T	E	R	I	F	R	I	E	D	I	W
P	L	Q	J	L	Z	N	H	S	I	F	L	D	M
S	R	E	M	D	R	E	D	N	A	I	R	O	C
B	L	A	M	O	H	A	K	Q	H	U	R	Y	U
E	A	L	W	O	T	P	W	C	C	N	M	A	Y
A	G	R	A	N	N	P	C	H	I	C	K	E	N
N	N	H	B	B	S	L	X	N	Y	L	G	C	T
G	U	C	G	E	T	E	G	R	M	I	R	U	G
T	G	A	R	R	C	A	R	Y	N	I	N	A	A
O	G	N	A	M	E	U	E	G	R	O	L	S	R
K	J	I	S	I	C	T	E	M	C	O	O	K	L
M	H	P	S	E	V	R	A	O	N	U	L	A	I
F	Y	S	R	I	C	E	C	W	R	B	P	G	C

✳ Only search for words that are in CAPITAL LETTERS. Two or more words in a phrase, like FINDERS KEEPERS, will usually be hidden separately in the grid.

130 **CODEWORD**

In this crossword, each letter of the alphabet appears as a code number. When you have replaced the decoded numbers with their letters in the grid, fill in the boxes at the bottom to reveal a saying or phrase.

25		9		22		19		17		9		15
1	24	14	9	12	19	25	9	15		1 **N**	4 **A**	22 **P**
23		9		4		15		9		6		4
4	13	1	25	1	16	15		15	5	17	19	15
1						17				25		8
19	4	22		25	1	9	20	22	9	26	19	
15		26		24				25		9		9
	21	24	13	1	19	17	26	1		21	25	8
15		3				1						7
18	1	9	9	12		7	24	1	4	1	2	4
25		10		25		24		9		4		15
26	24	19		14	4	26	25	9	19	25	9	15
19		15		9		1		21		12		11

A̶ B C D E F G H I J K L M N̶ O P̶ Q R S T U V W X Y Z̶

1 **N**	2	3	4 **A**	5	6	7	8	9	10	11	12	13
14	15	16	17	18	19	20	21	22 **P**	23	24	25	26

THE SAYING OR PHRASE IS:

15	24	17	26		16	26	4	22	9	15

131 **CROSSWORD**

Rearrange the letters in the shaded squares to spell out a fruit.

ACROSS

8 Chicken in a thick white sauce (9)

9 White wine and black currant drink (3)

10 Cold beverage (4,3)

11 Stocking fabric (5)

12 Notable age (3)

14 Short tale of an incident (8)

16 Old objects of value (8)

18 Without delay (3)

21 Fully grown (5)

23 Salad of diced apples, celery, and walnuts (7)

25 Of wines, dry (3)

26 Traditional and long-established in form or style (9)

DOWN

1 Place of business (6)

2 Small rodents (4)

3 Smoked and seasoned slices of beef (8)

4 Succeed in avoiding (6)

5 Tube carrying blood to the heart (4)

6 Complete set of bones (8)

7 New York borough north of Manhattan (5)

13 Make known publicly (8)

15 Make public (8)

17 Remove the packaging from (6)

19 Crisp batter cake (6)

20 Spicy tomato sauce or dip (5)

22 Fried tortilla (4)

24 In the past (4)

1 What does it mean to "bake the pastry blind"?

2 From what country do Edam and Gouda cheese come?

3 Buffalo wings are made from which animal?

4 Is white wine made from red or white grapes?

5 What is the name of the bar in *The Dukes of Hazzard*?

6 According to the Bible, which came first—the chicken or the egg?

7 Sometimes the orange coral (roe) is cooked with the white part of scallops, sometimes removed. Which is correct?

8 What is arrowroot made from and what is its most usual purpose?

MOBILE CODE

If PUMPKIN is 7867546 on this phone keypad, which FRUITS have the following numbers?

1 344

2 7586

3 243779

4 226262

5 5867828

134 COOL BOX

All these words are arranged in various box shapes in the grid.
One solution is shown.

A	G	I	C	E	C	T	S	A	N	D	C	C	O	P
C	H	S	E	B	U	R	H	C	I	W	P	D	L	L
E	E	N	V	J	D	G	T	F	O	B	N	U	I	L
S	E	W	D	F	R	O	J	D	O	D	S	D	T	H
P	G	V	B	Y	T	S	H	J	B	D	F	R	E	S
L	L	D	R	M	Y	T	R	G	N	Z	E	Z	E	P
L	I	N	I	N	X	C	M	G	L	K	E	Y	R	T
A	D	K	S	D	U	P	I	C	Y	P	E	P	R	V
B	V	C	B	K	J	C	I	N	D	C	O	G	D	S
J	Y	O	N	G	B	Y	R	E	O	L	O	S	U	Q
K	U	G	N	S	E	W	S	N	A	S	L	H	S	A
I	R	T	P	U	D	D	C	A	H	F	R	I	V	N
N	X	C	S	G	N	I	K	S	E	E	G	D	O	H
F	R	O	G	Y	Q	N	V	C	G	H	V	N	M	B
N	E	Z	J	E	R	F	C	S	D	U	R	P	F	L

CHEESE	FREEZE	ICE CUBES	SANDWICH
COLD	FRIDGE	~~KEEP COOL~~	SNACKS
DRINKS	FROSTY	PICNIC	YOGURT
FOOD	FROZEN	PUDDINGS	

In this crossword, each letter of the alphabet appears as a code number. When you have replaced the decoded numbers with their letters in the grid, fill in the boxes at the bottom to reveal a saying or phrase.

2	20	6	14	15		24	17	2	25	7	2	11
	22		26		22		2		7		1	
24	2	4	24	14	20	22	4		9	5	13	11
	4		11		4		22		20		22	
11	2	20	22	14	17		13	14	10	2	17	
			23		2		17				2	
16	22	20	2		9	18	14		11	9	11	12
	17				11		4		21			
	10	12	9	10	22		9	18	26	7	24	11
	11		19		20		7		9		2	
7	14	9	3		8	9	7	14	11	12	2	11
	5		26		7		15		12		24	
18	2	13	7	14	15	11		5	15 **Y**	24 **T**	12 **H**	11

A B C D E F G̸ I J K L M N O P Q R S̸ U V W X̸ Z

1	2	3	4	5	6	7	8	9	10	11	12 **H**	13
14	15 **Y**	16	17	18	19	20	21	22	23	24 **T**	25	26

THE SAYING OR PHRASE IS:

4	14	26	4	12		13	14	24	9	24	14

136 **ARROWORD**

The arrows show the direction in which the answer to each clue should be placed. When complete, rearrange the letters in the shaded squares to spell out a spice.

	▼		▼		▼		▼
Planetary moons		Spider's trap		Figure made by a sculptor		Space, universe	
▶				Van Gogh's painting medium		Sell	
Masculine gender		Wild pigs ▶		▼		▼	
▶			One thing ▶				
Look at		Canine friend of Mickey Mouse ▶					
▶			Large bodies of water ▶				
Small common insect		__ 66, popular song	▼	William __, famous Quaker	Unlawful act		Level betting odds
Thick, sticky syrup ▶		▼			▼		▼
▶				Go bad		__ Francisco, Californian city	
Illuminated sign gas	▶		▼			▼	
Adds sugar to	Break of day		Country bordering Saudi Arabia ▶				
▶							

143

Menu.

```
E  T  T  E  Z  U  S  E  Q  L  P  R  E  F
C  S  J  Y  F  X  U  S  E  O  R  U  H  I
O  R  I  O  B  G  U  S  M  R  O  E  C  L
N  C  U  A  N  O  I  I  M  R  V  S  I  E
S  R  O  I  D  A  M  A  V  A  E  S  U  T
O  E  R  U  N  N  D  B  S  I  N  A  Q  E
M  E  S  R  L  E  A  A  E  N  C  H  A  T
M  N  A  I  L  I  L  L  T  E  A  C  I  O
E  E  I  E  A  A  S  L  L  N  L  T  O  P
B  V  I  C  D  N  V  I  B  O  E  C  L  M
E  N  F  E  O  L  N  U  V  P  H  V  I  O
E  W  E  L  L  I  U  O  T  A  T  A  R  C
B  I  S  Q  U  E  S  B  Y  C  R  E  P  E
C  A  S  S  O  U  L  E  T  L  F  O  U  D
D  U  C  H  E  S  S  E  N  O  N  G  I  M
E  N  I  T  N  E  R  O  L  F  I  L  E  O
```

AIOLI	CONSOMME	MADELEINE
BEARNAISE	COULIS	MERINGUE
BISQUE	CREPE SUZETTE	PETIT FOUR
BOMBE	DUCHESSE	PROVENCAL
BOUILLABAISSE	FILET MIGNON	QUICHE LORRAINE
CASSOULET	FLORENTINE	RATATOUILLE
CHASSEUR	HOLLANDAISE	SALADE NICOISE
COMPOTE	LYONNAISE	VOL-au-VENT

✱ Only search for words that are in CAPITAL LETTERS. Two or more words in a
phrase, like FINDERS KEEPERS, will usually be hidden separately in the grid.

Fit the pieces in the grid to spell out a fruit in each row.

139 **WORDWHEEL**

Using only the letters in the wordwheel, you have ten minutes to find as many words as possible, none of which may be plurals, foreign words, or proper nouns. Each word must be of three letters or more, all must contain the central letter, and letters can only be used once in every word. There is at least one nine-letter word in the wheel.

- On the last Wednesday of August each year a massive tomato food fight is held on the streets of Buñol, Spain. This event is called La Tomatina.

- The reason for swirling wine in the glass is to allow more oxygen into it, which releases the aroma.

- In British English, the idiom "having the IQ of a turnip" is used to describe low intelligence or stupidity.

- Strawberries were considered poisonous in Argentina until the mid-nineteenth century.

- Pizza Planet is the name of the restaurant visited in *Toy Story*.

- Quiznos fast-food chain had a commercial featuring the singing rodents called "Sponge Monkeys."

- Years ago lobster was so plentiful it was referred to as a "poor man's food."

- Coca-Cola was the first soft drink to be consumed in outer space.

141 CROSSWORD

Rearrange the letters in the shaded squares to spell out a dessert (3,4,3).

ACROSS

1 Disorderly (6)
4 Looked to be (6)
9 Venezuelan or Ecuadorian, e.g. (5,8)
10 Box cover (3)
11 Fruit whose varieties include cantaloupe and galia (5)
13 No longer in the game (3)
14 Accuracy (5)
15 Richest part of milk (5)
19 Item in an auction (3)
20 ___ Berry, Oscar-winning actress (5)
21 Long slippery fish (3)
22 Cocktail-bar nibbles (7,6)
25 Using a garden tool (6)
26 Walt ___, creator of Mickey Mouse (6)

DOWN

1 Still in the shop (6)
2 Extremely surprised (13)
3 Homer Simpson's favorite exclamation (3)
5 Spike of corn (3)
6 Device for heating food quickly (9,4)
7 Give as a gift (6)
8 Slight, minor (5)
11 Sports fixture (5)
12 Firm self-control (5)
16 Nearer (to) (6)
17 Walks heavily (5)
18 Polished and shiny (6)
23 Aquatic animal's steering organ (3)
24 Hawaiian floral garland (3)

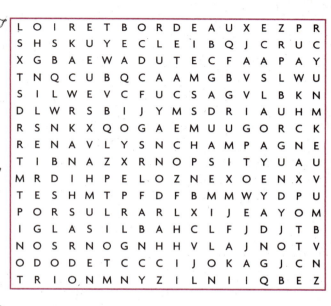

```
L O I R E T B O R D E A U X E Z P R
S H S K U Y E C L E I B Q J C R U C
X G B A E W A D U T E C F A A P A Y
T N Q C U B Q C A A M G B V S L W U
S I L W E V C F U C S A G V L B K N
D L W R S B I J Y M S D R I A U H M
R S N K X Q O G A E M U U G O R C K
R E N A V L Y S N C H A M P A G N E
T I B N A Z X R N O P S I T Y U A U
M R D I H P E L O Z N E X O E N X V
T E S H M T P F D F B M M W Y D P U
P O R S U L R A R L X I J E A Y O M
I G L A S I L B A H C L F J D J T B
N O S R N O G N H H V L A J N O T V
O D O D E T C C C I J O K A G J C N
T R I O N M N Y Z I L N I I Q B E Z
```

ALSACE	MEDOC
ANJOU	MERLOT
BEAUJOLAIS	MUSCADET
BORDEAUX	PAUILLAC
BURGUNDY	PINOT NOIR
CABERNET	RIESLING
CHABLIS	SAUTERNES
CHAMPAGNE	SAUVIGNON
CHARDONNAY	BLANC
LOIRE	SEMILLON
MARGAUX	SYLVANER

✶ Two or more words in a phrase, like
FINDERS KEEPERS, will usually be
hidden separately in the grid.

KRISS KROSS

See how quickly you can fit the listed words into the interlocking grid. The shaded squares will reveal a salad of raw vegetables.

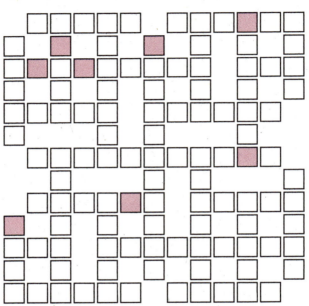

3 LETTERS
NAP
OUT

4 LETTERS
ESPY
WORM

5 LETTERS
ADORE
CRYPT
EAVES
LOSER
PRUDE
SHEAF
SITAR
SPACE
TWIST
WORDY

6 LETTERS
BUREAU
INFORM
MODEST
PSYCHE

7 LETTERS
ALLUDED
CENTRAL
ERUPTED
SKEPTIC

9 LETTERS
PERSECUTE
VALIDATED

11 LETTERS
LUDICROUSLY
MERCURIALLY

The arrows show the direction in which the answer to each clue should be placed. When complete, rearrange the letters in the shaded squares to spell out a fruit.

Tactful ▼		Vivacity ▼		Dutch flowers	Venice's country	Wearying overnight flight (3-3)	▼
►				▼	▼		
Duration of a person's existence		Set down ►				Nothing, nil	
►			Lie around ►			▼	
Every single one		__ Cyrus, teenage U.S. actress ►					
►			Funeral heap ►				
Unit of electrical current		Take on as your own	Low-down		Faults		Show to be false
Small label ►	▼		▼	Be keen on	▼	Back of the neck	▼
►				▼		▼	
Separate business enterprise ►							
May I have a look? (3,2,3)	Funnel-shaped		Flat-topped military hat ►				
►							

```
A  A  W  T  B  S  L  X  N  I  R  A  G  R  A  M  R
M  N  U  H  P  B  R  E  A  D  M  L  L  O  R  E  H
R  N  U  R  I  A  O  M  G  H  A  U  F  F  B  A  C
H  O  E  T  E  T  L  A  K  A  H  C  S  M  H  T  N
D  A  L  A  S  S  U  R  C  S  B  W  U  T  W  G  U
D  C  H  R  E  M  I  G  A  O  E  C  N  H  A  E  L
E  F  A  T  A  U  H  A  E  N  U  E  O  U  S  R  I
G  N  I  L  L  I  F  R  N  C  A  L  H  E  L  S  D
N  H  A  L  A  Q  O  I  R  N  E  R  E  C  M  L  B
W  S  B  O  L  S  P  N  B  M  O  H  G  U  W  I  U
K  B  A  B  Y  I  V  E  E  A  C  Y  S  C  R  C  T
B  A  K  E  R  Y  N  A  S  O  G  T  A  U  E  E  T
A  B  E  C  P  O  L  P  P  A  A  E  L  M  T  D  E
M  J  R  R  N  D  W  E  Y  R  L  X  A  B  T  T  E
S  P  R  E  A  G  N  N  B  R  E  A  V  E  U  L  G
B  L  P  S  I  C  H  I  C  K  E  N  M  N  B  G  D
H  A  I  S  G  C  H  I  C  K  E  S  Z  I  E  S  E
```

BAGEL	EGG	SALAD
BAKERY	FILLING	SALAMI
BREAD	HAM	SLICED
BROWN	LUNCH	SPREAD
BUTTER	MARGARINE	TUNA
CHEESE	MAYONNAISE	WHITE
CHICKEN	MUSTARD	WHOLE-MEAL
CRESS	OPEN	
CUCUMBER	ROLL	

146 CODEWORD

In this crossword, each letter of the alphabet appears as a code number. When you have replaced the decoded numbers with their letters in the grid, fill in the boxes at the bottom to reveal a saying or phrase.

16		6		26				12		17		1
18	8	13	15	24	18	25		14	18	15	16	24
19		15		12		18 **E**		4		23		15
9	14	4		20	22	4 **T**	16	9	10	18	16	4
20				25		16 **R**		6		4		
2	15	1	21	1		20	17	22	20	4	18	25
18		12				11				18		16
1	21	20	4	4	24	18		3	15	1	4	18
		4		18		22		20				1
1	4	15	17	22	15	4	18	1		2	9	1
15		3		9		15		18		13		18
14	15	24	18	16		24	15	2	5	12	18	16
1		7		1				4		11		1

A B C D ~~E~~ F G H I J K L M N O P Q ~~R~~ S ~~T~~ U V W X Y Z

1	2	3	4 **T**	5	6	7	8	9	10	11	12	13
14	15	16 **R**	17	18 **E**	19	20	21	22	23	24	25	26

THE SAYING OR PHRASE IS:

| 3 | 20 | 4 | 18 | | 9 | 26 | 26 | | 11 | 9 | 16 | 18 |

| 4 | 13 | 15 | 22 | | 7 | 9 | 12 | | 2 | 15 | 22 | | 2 | 13 | 18 | 6 |

Rearrange the letters in the shaded squares to spell out a cocktail (4,6).

ACROSS

1 Follow rapidly and try to catch (5)
4 Sediment that settles in drinks (5)
9 Permanently frozen Arctic plain (6)
10 Reluctant (6)
12 Champion of an Olympic event (4,9)
13 Forbidden (7)
18 Younger female relative (13)
19 Soil-turning farm implement (6)
20 Cosmetic liquid (6)
21 Middle of the body (5)
22 Wicked, heartless (5)

DOWN

2 Carrying-strap (6)
3 Accompaniment to tossed salads, in the theme song for the sitcom *Frasier* (9,4)
5 Partitioned entrance that turns (9,4)
6 Small, strong, onion-like bulb (6)
7 Actor's platform (5)
8 Italian sauce with basil and pine nuts (5)
11 Chief commander of a navy (7)
14 Land of the Pyramids (5)
15 Indian pastry filled with vegetables or meat (6)
16 Baseball term for a missed hit (6)
17 Foreground (5)

1 Colored and decorated eggs are a feature of Eastertime. Which nation first started decorating eggs?

2 We are urged to eat more fish but why are mackerel, herring, salmon, sardines, etc. especially good?

3 What topping is put on a steak to make it *au poivre*?

4 What cheese should be used in a classic Caesar salad?

5 What is Mexico's national drink?

6 How are peppers skinned?

7 What is the correct name for a Mexican filled pancake?

8 What important vitamin does rosehip syrup provide?

Can you fit the ten jigsaw pieces in the grid so that something you might find on a pizza appears down each of the seven columns?

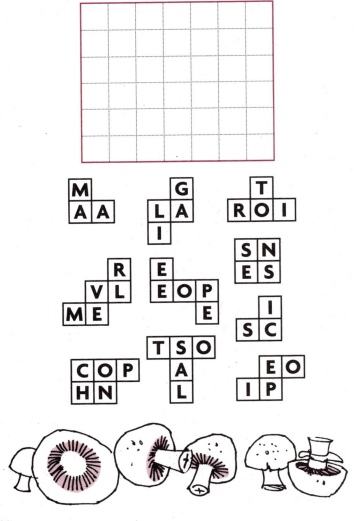

```
H T T C S Y R U J O T H L
C L N B H K R S N A A O H
R A A L I O P I K F H H H
E T T A L O C E F A C S Q
A T S C O C A O O B O E N
W Q N E U W F N L L M R U
D B I P A R A Z W A Y P O
V E P Y O E U H O C T S R
H A P T B M B C L K B E G
C I H P E R C O L A T O R
O N A C I R E M A U R C D
M S E W E H U K M S G N Z
  T T H S O W I H U U U
  A N I P M L O S O M L
  N A P R K F F R O M I
  Y W P E S U G A R E M
  B A E S N C P M F A S
  S E C S C O F F E E Y
  T K A O O T O R F D R
  I A F N A C C P L X U
  G T S S S E R P S E P
```

AMERICANO

BEANS

BLACK COFFEE

CAFE

CAPPUCCINO

CHOCOLATE

ESPRESSO

FROTH

GROUND

HOT MILK

INSTANT

LATTE

MARSHMALLOW

MOCHA

MUG

PERCOLATOR

SPOON

STIR

SUGAR

SYRUP

TAKE-AWAY

WHIPPED CREAM

✱ Two or more words in a phrase, like FINDERS KEEPERS, will usually be hidden separately in the grid.

KRISS KROSS

See how quickly you can fit the listed words into the interlocking grid. The shaded squares will reveal the name of a seafood dish.

5 LETTERS

CLOTH
FLAYS
KNEEL
SHAME
SPICE
STATE
STEER
TERSE

6 LETTERS

ACCUSE
ELAPSE
ENTAIL
IMMUNE
MAULED
MINUET
POUTED
TRUANT

7 LETTERS

HEARTHS
HORRIFY

13 LETTERS

CONSCIOUSNESS
HEMISPHERICAL
NONCONFORMIST
TREACHEROUSLY

152 WORDWHEEL

Using only the letters in the wordwheel, you have ten minutes to find as many words as possible, none of which may be plurals, foreign words, or proper nouns. Each word must be of three letters or more, all must contain the central letter, and letters can only be used once in every word. There is at least one nine-letter word in the wheel.

KITCHEN FRENCH

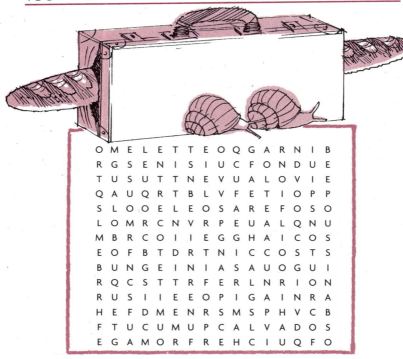

```
O M E L E T T E O Q G A R N I B
R G S E N I S I U C F O N D U E
T U S U T T N E V U A L O V I E
Q A U Q R T B L V F E T I O P P
S L O O E L E O S A R E F O S O
L O M R C N V R P E U A L Q N U
M B R C O I I E G G H A I C O S
E O F B T D R T N I C C O S T S
B U N G E I N I A S A U O G U I
R Q C S T T R F E R L N R I O N
R U S I I E E O P I G A I N R A
H E F D M E N R S M S P H V C B
F T U C U M U P C A L V A D O S
E G A M O R F R E H C I U Q F O
```

APERITIF
BOUQUET GARNI
BRIOCHE
CALVADOS
COULIS
CROQUE
  MONSIEUR
CROUTONS
CUISINE
ENTRECOTE
ESCALOPE
FOIE GRAS

FONDUE
FROMAGE
  FRAIS
GRATIN
MERINGUE

MOUSSE
OMELETTE
POUSSIN
PROFITEROLE
QUICHE
SORBET
VINAIGRETTE
VOL-AU-VENT

✱ Two or more words in a phrase, like FINDERS KEEPERS, will usually be hidden
separately in the grid.

154 **CODEWORD**

In this crossword, each letter of the alphabet appears as a code number. When you have replaced the decoded numbers with their letters in the grid, fill in the boxes at the bottom to reveal a saying or phrase.

8	21	1	1	25	18	20		26	22	7	18	16
	3		7		7		1		3		21	
13	23	21	24	7	13	7	25	19	21	10	10	16
	21		24		3		12				4	
26	13	16	10	7	26	13	26		5	10	3	15
	3		3				26		7		26	
		3	1	3	23	6	3	19	18	16		
	7		3		3				13		9	
21	19	25	19		18	21	22	26	7	11	3	26
	2				25		3		25		10	
17	12	3	26	13	7	25	19	7	19 **N**	6	10	16
	23		22		10		18		21 **A**		3	
9	16	14	21	16		23	3	21	10 **L**	7	26	13

A B C D E F G H I J K L M N O P Q R S T U V W X Y Z

1	2	3	4	5	6	7	8	9	10 **L**	11	12	13
14	15	16	17	18	19 **N**	20	21 **A**	22	23	24	25	26

THE SAYING OR PHRASE IS:

21	22	22	10	3		25	5		1	16		3	16	3

Try solving this logic problem in your head before putting pen to paper.

Three couples were dining out on St. Valentine's Day. From the information below, match up each couple, say which type of restaurant they dined out at, and how they met.

Alex and Ashley met on vacation, and went to a restaurant serving the cuisine of the country where they met. Pat insisted on going to a Thai restaurant, but not with Sam. Jo, an accountant, was not the person who met Les (who dined at an Indian restaurant) at the office, and the couple dining at the French restaurant did not meet at the gym.

- Winnie the Pooh's favorite food is honey.

- Spuds Mackenzie was a mascot for Bud Light beer.

- Mateus Rose wine comes from Portugal.

- Food idioms include "rotten apple," "big cheese," "pinch of salt," "eat humble pie," "like peas in a pod," "sour grapes," "couch potato," "in a nutshell," "upset the applecart," "smell fishy," "bad egg," and "gravy train."

- Dandelions, pansies, and sunflowers are all edible.

- The first product with a barcode to be scanned at a checkout was a pack of Wrigley's Juicy Fruit chewing gum.

- In the United States, a pound of potato chips costs two hundred times more than a pound of potatoes.

- The diner in *Saved by the Bell* is called The Max.

CROSSWORD

Rearrange the letters in the shaded squares to spell out a salad vegetable.

ACROSS

7 Small lump of gold (6)
8 Rough, husky (6)
9 Fruit related to the apple (4)
10 Steal from (3)
11 Pleasant, enjoyable (4)
12 Looked happy (6)
14 Ship's brake (6)
16 Prolonged anxiety (6)
19 Frankfurter in a bun (3,3)
21 Scuttling shellfish (4)
23 Gases inside the atmosphere (3)
24 Walker's route (4)
25 Plant with aromatic seeds (6)
26 Outer coating of a tooth (6)

DOWN

1 Building housing historic items (6)
2 Food thickener from seaweed (4)
3 Watched, gazed (6)
4 Irrational fear (6)
5 Smooth grassy area beside a house (4)
6 Classic Hitchcock thriller (6)
13 False statement (3)
15 Divide into pieces with a knife (3)
17 Poultry bird (6)
18 Salt dispenser (6)
19 ___ Globetrotters, famous basketball team (6)
20 Beginning (6)
22 High-fiber part of grain (4)
24 High point (4)

```
            C Y E L P R C P I G
          U P T L O S U E I H E K H U
        E E N P O E N F H P R I N C E W
      T S E L T U N R F S S F R C M B I M
      F L Y S D G C I B U T O G O K O G G
    D P E D D O D Y F A L H G R Y D E R P W
    U O A L V C H A M L B Y E I W W I N L O
    K O O Y L Y A T S L E L H T A S P R T O
    T M W H U E M U S H R O O M E N V N E D
    S D A Y R D R L N P S I B T P R T K V S
    A T I N A M A E O B C C T R U S S U L A
    B O B C W W L L T H O E A T Y R K W E I
    O O C E Y F O E T N R L S R E A B E V D
    N F F E F D V H U A A K E L L L G E B N
    N N R U P N W C B A V H L T E E L P R D
    E S R O V C I R A G A I C W E I T I L W
    T T F A I R Y O U B M E I F O M G N T B
    V U S F L C F L D M H T W O D I W G A G
```

AMANITA

BLEWIT

BLUSHER

BOLETE

BONNET

CEP

CHANTERELLE

CHICKEN of the WOODS

DRYAD'S SADDLE

ELF-CUP

FAIRY BUTTON

FLY AGARIC

GIANT PUFFBALL

GRISETTE

HORN of PLENTY

LAWYER'S WIG

LORCHEL

MILLER

MOREL

MUSH-ROOM

PRINCE

RUSSULA

SCARLET HOOD

TOADSTOOL

TRUFFLE

VELVET FOOT

WEEPING WIDOW

✳ Only search for words that are in CAPITAL LETTERS. Two or more words in a phrase, like FINDERS KEEPERS, will usually be hidden separately in the grid.

KRISS KROSS

See how quickly you can fit the listed words into the interlocking grid. The shaded squares will reveal a spice.

4 LETTERS

DADO
EARN

5 LETTERS

ADORN
DETER
EDICT
ESSAY
LATER
WIDOW

6 LETTERS

ACHING
COMMIT
CORNEA
DEBTOR
DUCKED
ENTOMB
SKATER
UNEASE

7 LETTERS

CORDIAL
COUNTRY
CULLING
NEIGHED
QUASHED
SITUATE
STARLIT
VENTURE

9 LETTERS

DEVOURING

160 **ARROWORD**

The arrows show the direction in which the answer to each clue should be placed. When complete, rearrange the letters in the shaded squares to spell out a type of grape used to make wine (5,4).

Salad dressing, informally	▼	Strong wind	▼	Mountaineer (4,7)	▼	Entertained, delighted	Occasion of public visiting (4,3)
►				Inner self ►			▼
Look for		Tooth on a wheel ►				__ Collette, Australian actress	
►				Dined ►		▼	
American __, talent show	Educational certificate	Double-dot punctuation mark ►					
►	▼			Finish ►			
Electronic junk mail		Country bordering Pakistan ►					
►				Revise for the press	Political adviser	Old torn cloth	
Joke-telling entertainer		Large furry animal ►		▼	▼	▼	Trawler's fish trap
►							▼
Cooking grease		Narrow top or crest ►					
►			Experiment ►				

APRON
BAKING
BARBECUING
BASTING
BLANCHING
BOILING
BRAISING
BROILING
BROWNING
CARAMELIZING
CASSEROLE
CHEF
CODDLING
CUISINE
CURING
CURRY
DEEP-FRYING
FRICASSEE
GRIDDLING

GRILLING
HEAT
INGREDIENTS
KITCHEN
MARINADE
MARINATING
MICROWAVE
OVEN-ROASTING
PICKLING
POACHING
POT-ROASTING
POTS and PANS
PRESSURE-
  COOKER
RECIPE
REDUCING
SAUCE
SAUTEING
SCRAMBLING
SIMMERING

SLOW-COOKING
SMOKING
SPIT-ROASTING
STEAMING
STEWING
STIR-FRYING

STOVE
TANDOORI
TENDERIZING
THICKENING
TOASTING

✱ Only search for words that are in CAPITAL LETTERS. Two or more words in a phrase, like FINDERS KEEPERS, will usually be hidden separately in the grid.

```
S P M I C R O W A V E B G G R S A U C F S
S R E C I H E A P R M N A P N O A O B L G
P I D E O R P K D V I T X R L I D U O C N
I Y M C U R R Y O T R A Y A B D M W C A I
N S I M O U P T S O E E E U L E C A R E K
G G E N E C S A T G C H D I C O C P E H A
R N S H G R O E O N U E N U O G A U C T B
E I I Z C R I R V I R G R K C N W P I N S
D H G L N T E N E Z I R I U X I O O P N I
I C E E K D I D G I S N S T S T N T W R G
E A V A U C G K I L G A A H T S T P G N S
N O V C Y N I M A E T S U I O A E N I T K
T P I P O T G P U M N A C C V O I R E F S
Q N I H C N A L B A Q T F K I T U W P T J
G N I H C N A L B R Y A S E A C I C I O A
P C E S P I T R O A S T I N G N H R B P E
R N B A S T I N G C B G I I U E F B R L B
E A R U H N A P P C U R I N P R S T O P O
S P O T E D A N O L A S O G Y C P R W B I
S F W E E N T P T M D Q E I H P E A N A L
U G N I T S A O R T O P N E L S F I I K I
R J I N G M N K O E G G A B S I T G N I N
E I C G N O D O A N N L H A B S N A G N G
C R G N I K O M S D I S C R A I A G K N G
O U I P L I O W T E L M I B W K Q C N N Z
O C I X D N R C I R B D E E P F R Y I N G
K A K S D H U M N I M V T C P E J L K R H
E D A N I R A M A Z A S W U C I L O A T F
V Z B O R N C R N I R U C I Z I C C B E O
E R C J G U E H W N C Z P K R T T E H L C
B R A I S I N G E G S X B G B V M C R E J
S C R A M B L I N Q I R O O D N A T X H L
```

162 **CROSSWORD**

Rearrange the letters in the shaded squares to spell out a grape used in wine making (8,9).

ACROSS

3 Egyptian tasseled hat (3)

7 Permanent picture on the skin (6)

8 Mass migration (6)

9 Without sound (6)

10 Public protest (6)

11 Alley sport (6,7)

13 Crisp vegetable often used in Chinese dishes (5,8)

18 Cocktail with rum, sugar, lime, and mint (6)

19 Formally charge (6)

20 Zodiac twins (6)

21 Fruit with a morello variety (6)

22 Location of the iris (3)

DOWN

1 Narrow steep-sided valley (6)

2 Meryl ___, *Mamma Mia!* star (6)

3 Cookie with a prediction or motto in it (7,6)

4 Refusal to accept any bad behavior (4,9)

5 Lodging place (6)

6 Charity race (3,3)

11 Pull (another vehicle) (3)

12 Understand (3)

14 Loved very much (6)

15 Magic potion (6)

16 Pass card (6)

17 Not able to decide (6)

163 FOOD QUIZ

1 Cornstarch has a different name in Britain. What is it?

2 In what way are eggs prepared for eggs Benedict?

3 In Indian cooking, "ghee" is frequently mentioned. What is this?

4 What are fleurons?

5 Big Boy, Plum, and Beefsteak are varieties of what?

6 What is the best way to dissolve leaf or powdered gelatin?

7 What is Biltong?

8 What kind of rice should be used in a risotto?

In this crossword, each letter of the alphabet appears as a code number. When you have replaced the decoded numbers with their letters in the grid, fill in the boxes at the bottom to reveal a saying or phrase.

11	7	3	2	1	12	22	3		15	7	13	20
	3		17		13		17		20		11	
21	5	3	7	15	21		7	3	8	5	3	25
	15				26				5		20	
20	3	23	24	7	13	13	10		1	22	5	9
	8		23		7		15		3		9	
		12	3	26	17	15	5	15	20	22		
	14		17		26		5 L		19		17	
26	1	8	26		3	9	3 E	11	17	26	21	16
	13		6				20 N				26	
17	26	26	17	21	16		20	17	11	4	15	20
	3		20		17		15		15		20	
1	24	3	12		24	21	17	18	3	20	22	3

A B C D E̶ F G H I J K L̶ M N̶ O P Q R S T U V W X Y Z

1	2	3 E	4	5 L	6	7	8	9	10	11	12	13
14	15	16	17	18	19	20 N	21	22	23	24	25	26

THE SAYING OR PHRASE IS:

22	7	17	18	9		26	7	17	15	20

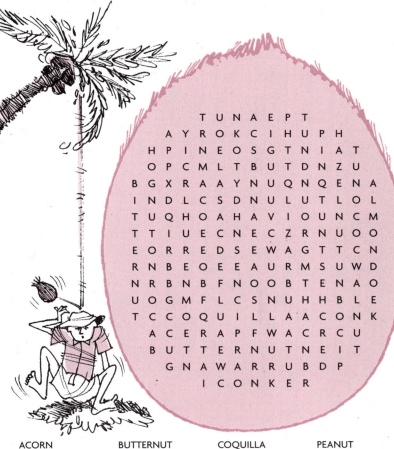

```
            T U N A E P T
          A Y R O K C I H U P H
        H P I N E O S G T N I A T
        O P C M L T B U T D N Z U
      B G X R A A Y N U Q N Q E N A
      I N D L C S D N U L U T L O L
      T U Q H O A H A V I O U N C M
      T T I U E C N E C Z R N U O O
      E O R R E D S E W A G T T C N
      R N B E O E E A U R M S U W D
      N R B N B F N O O B T E N A O
      U O G M F L C S N U H H B L E
      T C C O Q U I L L A A C O N K
        A C E R A P F W A C R C U
        B U T T E R N U T N E I T
        G N A W A R R U B D P
            I C O N K E R
```

ACORN	BUTTERNUT	COQUILLA	PEANUT
ALMOND	CASHEW	FILBERT	PECAN
ARECA	CHESTNUT	GROUND-NUT	PINE
BEECHNUT	COBNUT		PISTACHIO
BITTERNUT	COCONUT	HAZELNUT	QUANDONG
BRAZIL	COFFEE	HICKORY	QUEENSLAND
BREADNUT	COLA	HOGNUT	SAOUARI
BURRAWANG	CONKER	MACADAMIA	WALNUT

KRISS KROSS

See how quickly you can fit the listed words into the interlocking grid. The shaded squares will reveal the name of a sandwich.

4 LETTERS

ASTI
NUDE

5 LETTERS

ADAPT
DOZEN
GRASS
INANE
KILLS
STRAP

6 LETTERS

EYEING
HUNTER
OOZING
PAELLA
PANELS
REARED
SOLELY
STYLUS

7 LETTERS

BLUNTLY
DELVING
NETTLED
ODDNESS
POULTRY
SUCKING
VERANDA
WILDCAT

9 LETTERS

PANDERING

The arrows show the direction in which the answer to each clue should be placed. When complete, rearrange the letters in the shaded squares to spell out a dessert.

Lack, deficiency	▼	Tree affected by "Dutch" disease	▼		Hoisted	▼	Australian tree-climbing "bear"	Land for building on
__ Dolly, 1969 musical				▼			Bart Simpson's mom	▼
Cook in oil		Popular resort city in Florida ▶					▼	
▶			Of a battery, expired ▶					
Electronically transmitted document		Fixed gaze ▶						
▶			Unwell		Trader			Moved to music
Himalayan Bigfoot		Summed up ▶	▼		▼			▼
▶				Old Testament priest		Compete to be first		
Pink __, Natalie Cole song	Section of a play	Fix (facts) in the mind ▶		▼		▼		
▶	▼							
Antlered male animal		Your nephew's sister ▶						
▶				Boston __ Sox, baseball team ▶				

APRON	DRINKS	MASHING	SERVING
BAKING	EDIBLE	MEALS	SIMMERING
BARBECUE	FARE	MEAT	SMOKING
BOILING	FISH	MIXING	SNACKS
BOWLS	FREEZER	NUTRITION	SOUFFLE
BRAISING	FRICASSEE	OVEN	SPICES
BREAD	FRIDGE	PANS	STEAMING
BREAKFAST	FROZEN FOOD	PANTRY	STEWING
CASSEROLE	FRUIT	PASTA	STIRRING
CODDLING	FRYING	PICKLING	STOVE
CONDIMENTS	GRILLING	POACHING	SUPPER
COOKER	HERBS	PREPARATION	SUSTENANCE
CROCKERY	HUNGRY	PROVISIONS	TINNED
CUISINE	KITCHEN	PUDDINGS	TOASTING
CUPBOARDS	LARDER	PUREE	TRAY
CURING	LUNCH	RICE	UTENSILS
DAIRY PRODUCE	MARINADE	ROASTING	VEGETABLES
DESSERTS	MARINATING	SCRAMBLING	
DINNER			

✳ Two or more words in a phrase, like FINDERS KEEPERS, will usually be hidden separately in the grid.

```
C G N I K O M S G S P G N I V R E S O B B
E A D O O F R S E T S R F R I D G J R F G
L A S F A E M L T N D I O P U R E E O N B
B V O S P T B E F E R C R V F D A N I T F
I G N P E A A R D M A T N A I K R R N R S
D G U I T R U E X I O M R N F S E I Y I E
E S N E S I O S M D B E I A I M I I N U T
X S G I T I F L S N P L S N M T N O C K F
D E E F L R U A E O U T Y I G G S E N O S
V B P R O D U C E C C R S H W O B U C S K
Y Z O Z V T D S R N D A E R B R R T O P C
D R E W E I L O E S O D Y N A G E E O C A
T N T E L A N V C U D I I B N N H N K N N
S O I N E S O L P S A N T R X I N S E A S
H N A M A R I N A T I N G A T T D I R N S
G U K S A P R O N E R E P I R S A L I E F
C N N I T I R T U N M L A S A A G S C T R
O S I G N I L B M A R C S I Y O P I N S I
N O S H R F N T F N N P T N Z R P E E U D
D U K S C J P G A C U S Q G E S I F R S G
I F R I C A S S E E T S G N I D D U P P E
M F R F Y C O O H E R B T M I C U D O R P
E L Q E R U P P W H I B A R W G U O V E B
N E S T E A M I N W T R F D A N I R A M J
T H C V K Z N T E S I G N I X I M P I E G
M N O M C G E T T N O G R I L L I N G N C
H T E T O P S R A G N I L K C I R P I U G
S C R H R A E D I B L N D Y L O V H I Q U
P A N S C S E O S S A C I R F B S S I C M
I C W U S T I R R I N G U I R A I K I I E
R I Y E L A I H U N G R Y A M N A Z O R F
R E D R A L W K N I R D A D E B A K I N G
```

VOWEL PLAY

Add the same vowel—more than once if required—to the following to spell out six items to eat.

1 C R B   **4** S L D

2 P S T   **5** L F L F

3 B N N   **6** P P Y

- SpongeBob SquarePants's favorite food is Krabby burgers.

- Arachibutyrophobia is the fear of peanut butter sticking to the roof of your mouth.

- Ambiguous food names include Bombay duck, buffalo wings, hamburger, and hot dog.

- A peach was the first fruit to be eaten on the moon.

- Drinking red wine in moderation has health benefits.

- Sandra Bullock, Bill Cosby, and Bruce Willis have all had former jobs as bartenders.

- White vinegar makes a good cleaning agent.

- Tony the Tiger is a mascot for Kellogg's.

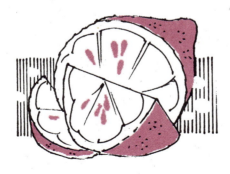

WORD LADDER

Change one letter at a time (but not the position of any letter) to make a new word—and move from the word at the top of the box to the word at the bottom, using the exact number of rungs provided.

B E E R

W I N E

```
S A P A T G Z W S O R B E T
E H C I U Q R S A M O S A F
O Z I R O H C A P L A E D F
G R A V L A X H T V D P F E
A N T I P A S T O I R O I L
N O T G N I L L E W N L R F
U T A K D M V M A A K A C F
K S I O O A O L G R L C H U
E E I U P U L O V I D S O O
V P S M S E R A L S G E W S
U S Y S A T Q T S O S K D U
E B A P S R C S J T R I E S
W K N E K C I H C T E E R H
A F O N D U E T G O E M N I
```

MOUSSE
PAELLA
PAVLOVA
PESTO
QUICHE
RISOTTO
SAMOSA
SORBET
SOUFFLE
STROGANOFF
SUSHI
TAPAS
TIRAMISU
WALDORF SALAD
WELLINGTON

ANTIPASTO
CHICKEN KIEV
CHORIZO

CHOWDER
ESCALOPE
FONDUE

GRATIN
GRAVLAX
MOUSSAKA

✱ Two or more words in a phrase, like FINDERS KEEPERS, will usually be hidden separately in the grid.

KRISS KROSS

See how quickly you can fit the listed words into the interlocking grid. The shaded squares will reveal fairground food.

4 LETTERS
CAPE
TRAY

5 LETTERS
ALIBI
EMAIL
ICIER
PLUMB
RIPER
UMBRA

6 LETTERS
AGENDA
INDOOR
INROAD
PYTHON

7 LETTERS
ANODYNE
AWFULLY
CAPTAIN
GIMMICK
HALVING
MOURNED
ORIGAMI
REFRAIN

12 LETTERS
COMMUNICATED
IRRITATINGLY
MARRIAGEABLE
UNPARALLELED

174 **ARROWORD**

The arrows show the direction in which the answer to each clue should be placed. When complete, rearrange the letters in the shaded squares to spell out a breakfast dish (4,6).

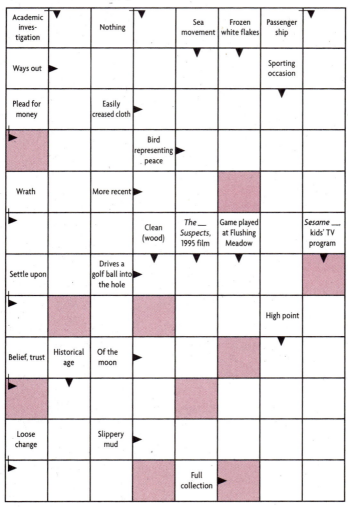

Academic investigation ▼		Nothing ▼		Sea movement	Frozen white flakes	Passenger ship	▼
Ways out ▶				▼	▼	Sporting occasion	
Plead for money		Easily creased cloth	▶			▼	
▶			Bird representing peace	▶			
Wrath		More recent	▶				
▶			Clean (wood)	The __ Suspects, 1995 film	Game played at Flushing Meadow		Sesame __, kids' TV program
Settle upon		Drives a golf ball into the hole	▶ ▼	▼	▼		▼
▶						High point	
Belief, trust	Historical age	Of the moon	▶			▼	
▶	▼						
Loose change		Slippery mud	▶				
▶				Full collection	▶		

175 · PACKED LUNCH

There are thirty LUNCHes hidden in this grid, one for each member of the class! Can you find them all?

176 **CODEWORD**

In this crossword, each letter of the alphabet appears as a code number. When you have replaced the decoded numbers with their letters in the grid, fill in the boxes at the bottom to reveal a saying or phrase.

7	25	22	12		12	6	13	11	10	13	13	25
	7		6		23		10		20		20	
23	12	1	20 **A**	22	23		7	21	26	13	10	21
	22		25 **M**		5		18		26			
14	15	13	22 **P**		12	22	20	1	7	13	8	12
	20		13				25				21	
20	1	10	13	26	20	9	7	1	20	15	15	4
	23				26				25		23	
20	12	12	23	12	12	23	12		20	3	20	10
			2		13		6		16		12	
19	23	21	7	20	15		20	15	7	18	6	9
	25		15		17		14		21		23	
24	8	7	23	9	23	12	9		18	13	19	12

A̶ B C D E F G H I J K L M̶ N O P̶ Q R S T U V W X Y Z

1	2	3	4	5	6	7	8	9	10	11	12	13
14	15	16	17	18	19	20 **A**	21	22 **P**	23	24	25 **M**	26

THE SAYING OR PHRASE IS:

14	15	20	12	6		7	21		9	6	23		22	20	21

185

177 **CROSSWORD**

Rearrange the letters in the shaded squares to spell out a pizza topping.

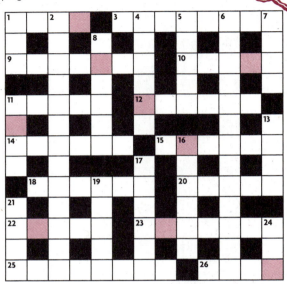

ACROSS

- **1** Leap (4)
- **3** Bark of a S.E. Asian tree, used as a spice (8)
- **9** Have admiration for (7)
- **10** Strong winds (5)
- **11** Enchant (5)
- **12** Public sign (6)
- **14** Paste made from ground sesame seeds (6)
- **15** Cuisine similar to Cajun (6)
- **18** Make certain (6)
- **20** Off-white wedding-dress color (5)
- **22** Took part in an election (5)
- **23** Popeye's vegetable (7)
- **25** Inhabitant (8)
- **26** Military truck (4)

DOWN

- **1** Glass container (3)
- **2** U.S. state that includes Martha's Vineyard (13)
- **4** Purposeful (6)
- **5** Time when we sleep (5)
- **6** Light brown confection (4,9)
- **7** Bird's shelter (4)
- **8** Talk based on a passage from the Bible (6)
- **11** Large town (4)
- **13** Exceedingly (4)
- **16** Dried fruit used in cake making (6)
- **17** Add condiments to (6)
- **19** Opened (a parcel) (5)
- **21** Remaining (4)
- **24** Thigh joint (3)

1 Pegasus, Alice, Sophie, and Emily are varieties of what?

2 What fish is used in the dish raie au beurre noir?

3 "Bangers" in Britain are what in the U.S.?

4 What is the name of the coffee shop in *Friends*?

5 Chives are frequently used in cooking. What are they and what is their flavor?

6 How does buckwheat differ from ordinary wheat?

7 How do you make croustades?

8 One of the best-known quiches is a quiche Lorraine. What are two of the ingredients used to flavor the filling?

179 **WORD LADDER**

Change one letter at a time (but not the position of any letter) to make a
new word—and move from the word at the top of the box to the word at the
bottom, using the exact number of rungs provided.

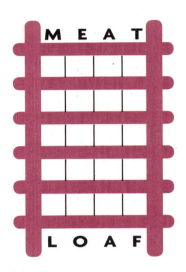

M E A T

L O A F

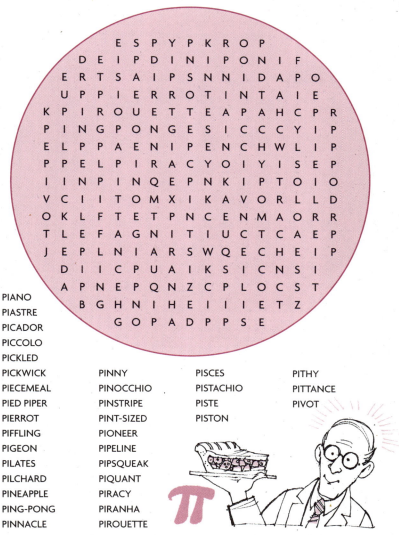

```
        E S P Y P K R O P
      D E I P D I N I P O N I F
    E R T S A I P S N N I D A P O
    U P P I E R R O T I N T A I E
  K P I R O U E T T E A P A H C P R
  P I N G P O N G E S I C C C Y I P
  E L P P A E N I P E N C H W L I P
  P P E L P I R A C Y O I Y I S E P
  I I N P I N Q E P N K I P T O I O
  V C I I T O M X I K A V O R L L D
  O K L F T E T P N C E N M A O R R
  T L E F A G N I T I U C T C A E P
  J E P L N I A R S W Q E C H E I P
  D I I C P U A I K S I C N S I
  A P N E P Q N Z C P L O C S T
    B G H N I H E I I I E T Z
      G O P A D P P S E
```

PIANO
PIASTRE
PICADOR
PICCOLO
PICKLED
PICKWICK
PIECEMEAL
PIED PIPER
PIERROT
PIFFLING
PIGEON
PILATES
PILCHARD
PINEAPPLE
PING-PONG
PINNACLE

PINNY
PINOCCHIO
PINSTRIPE
PINT-SIZED
PIONEER
PIPELINE
PIPSQUEAK
PIQUANT
PIRACY
PIRANHA
PIROUETTE

PISCES
PISTACHIO
PISTE
PISTON

PITHY
PITTANCE
PIVOT

✱ Two or more words in a phrase, like FINDERS KEEPERS, will usually be hidden
separately in the grid.

PATHFINDER

Beginning with the S in the square box, follow a continuous path to find 23 fruits and vegetables. The trail passes through each and every letter once, and may twist up, down, or sideways, but never diagonally.

S	O	Y	E	W	A	T	E	R	M	E	L	O
P	N	B	C	E	N	O	T	A	I	R	P	N
U	A	E	U	C	T	A	O	T	C	K	L	Y
M	P	T	T	N	I	R	P	E	T	O	E	P
I	K	E	L	E	A	N	G	L	A	R	A	R
N	J	R	I	C	M	I	O	P	P	R	A	A
L	A	P	A	O	I	N	T	O	M	A	C	S
A	P	L	E	T	H	C	S	E	P	T	O	P
N	E	A	K	Z	U	C	Q	U	U	N	A	A
O	R	E	D	P	L	L	E	A	O	T	C	R
W	S	P	P	E	C	H	B	S	L	A	S	A
E	R	E	R	N	A	E	P	H	H	E	U	G
E	T	C	O	O	N	I	O	N	C	R	R	Y

APPLE	LETTUCE	RED KALE
APRICOT	MANGO	SOYBEAN
ASPARAGUS	NECTARINE	SQUASH
BELL PEPPER	ONION	SWEET CORN
CANTALOUPE	PEACH	TOMATO
CARROT	POTATO	WATERMELON
CHERRY	PRICKLY PEAR	ZUCCHINI
JALAPENO	PUMPKIN	

The arrows show the direction in which the answer to each clue should be placed. When complete, rearrange the letters in the shaded squares to spell out a vegetable.

Person seeking excitement ▼	▼	Fish said to be slippery	▼	__ Royale, Bond movie	▼	Leave stranded	▼
►				__ Sandler, Spanglish actor		Hold (someone's attention)	
Outer border		Intensified light beam ►		▼		▼	
►			Fred Flintstone's pet ►				
That woman		Fleshy tropical fruit ►					
►			Grumble, complain				
Pen for keeping pigs		Drama set to music	▼	Knocks sharply	Small bits of land		Had a nap
Rock group's crew ►	▼				▼		▼
►				Personal		Neckline shape	
Surname of Jack Sparrow actor Johnny ►				▼		▼	
Model railway (5,3)	Make clear, settle		Shed tears ►				
►							

```
L E R E N N I D A R T N U O C
E H N W I N I Y T P S H O R T
I O S G J B R E C N A M O R H
S T C H A T E A U F F P S O O
U E Y Y N P S B O S K N W O L
R B R U R E M U S V A E W U I
E E O V S U R A O D E B O Z D
L C L O I P X O H K R P Z T A
E W R A O C R U E C B U Q R Y
T I S S X M E N L S C P O O H
O K T P O I D O W A O R P F U
H E X R R Z N A J I O R O M X
R E T R E A T G P O N M O O U
R E L A X I N L M S D E L C L
```

BREAKFAST in BED	HOTEL	ROOM SERVICE
CHAMPAGNE	JACUZZI	ROSES
CHATEAU	LEISURE	SHORT HOLIDAY
COMFORT	LUXURY	SPA
COUNTRY RETREAT	POOL	WEEKEND
DINNER	RELAXING	WINE
FOUR-POSTER	ROMANCE	

✳ Only search for words that are in CAPITAL LETTERS. Two or more words in a
phrase, like FINDERS KEEPERS, will usually be hidden separately in the grid.

184 **CODEWORD**

In this crossword, each letter of the alphabet appears as a code number. When you have replaced the decoded numbers with their letters in the grid, fill in the boxes at the bottom to reveal a saying or phrase.

	13	10	24	21 **B**	13		24	21	19	13	13	
23		24		11 **U**		10		11		24		6
8	24	15		13 **S**	12	11	7	25		21	8	8
13		22				21				2		2
9	8	13	23		14	24	10		4	22	24	2
7			8	1	22		23	8	22			24
10	8	26	1		24		22		1	11	16	21
24			22	2	16		3	2	11			8
2	7	22	25		13	24	10		22	16	7	14
7		17				3				24		24
10	22	24		6	14	24	18	19		5	11	10
19		16		24		14		24		8		22
	11	13	7	1	20		13	16	7	14	15	

A Ⱥ C D E F G H I J K L M N O P Q R Ş T Ʉ V W X Y Z

1	2	3	4	5	6	7	8	9	10	11 **U**	12	13 **S**
14	15	16	17	18	19	20	21 **B**	22	23	24	25	26

THE SAYING OR PHRASE IS:

21	14	7	1	20		23	8	16	22		10	23	22

21	24	6	8	1

Using only the letters in the wordwheel, you have ten minutes to find as many words as possible, none of which may be plurals, foreign words, or proper nouns. Each word must be of three letters or more, all must contain the central letter, and letters can only be used once in every word. There is at least one nine-letter word in the wheel.

- The bar in *Family Guy* is called the Drunken Clam.

- The dent in the bottom of a wine bottle is called a "punt." It can also be known as a "kick" or "kick-up."

- Mr. Peanut is the advertising logo and mascot of Planters.

- Apples are better at waking you up in the morning than coffee is.

- Ketchup was once sold as a medicine.

- The first Pizza Hut was built in Wichita, Kansas.

- McDonald's fast-food chain features a yearly Monopoly promotion.

- Methyphobia is the fear of alcohol.

Rearrange the letters in the shaded squares to spell out a type of sauce.

ACROSS

- **7** Salad relish (6)
- **8** Task involving a short journey (6)
- **9** Animal with a trunk (8)
- **10** From Monday to Sunday (4)
- **11** Measurement of surface (4)
- **12** Greatly surprise, amaze (8)
- **14** Oily fish, often smoked (8)
- **16** Hours, minutes (4)
- **18** Give off (fumes) (4)
- **20** Baseball-like game (8)
- **22** Dish between the fish and meat courses (6)
- **23** Tied up (a boat) (6)

DOWN

- **1** Post, column (6)
- **2** Tuna variety (8)
- **3** Greek goats' milk cheese (4)
- **4** Abstaining from alcohol (8)
- **5** Make (beer) (4)
- **6** Enrages (6)
- **12** Taken into custody (8)
- **13** Small writing pad (8)
- **15** Nut used to make marzipan (6)
- **17** Grain-flavored (6)
- **19** Change direction (4)
- **21** Stardom (4)

```
S  W  E  E  C  S  V  S  I  F  S  A  L  A  Z
D  E  S  S  E  R  T  E  R  Q  S  A  L  A  D
S  T  A  R  T  E  R  I  J  E  N  O  U  M  B
D  N  O  N  A  G  E  V  S  A  T  D  U  C  A
T  E  N  U  T  R  I  T  I  O  N  R  I  F  E
I  Z  S  S  O  U  L  R  F  S  V  E  A  W  R
U  O  U  S  D  B  A  C  T  E  C  A  G  T  B
R  R  Y  I  E  T  I  E  G  U  H  D  E  V  S
F  F  E  R  E  R  E  E  P  P  O  Y  V  R  A
J  T  X  G  I  W  T  G  G  U  C  H  S  I  F
S  Y  E  A  S  A  S  S  O  B  O  R  K  H  M
D  V  D  B  B  L  D  R  S  R  L  S  I  E  T
O  I  S  L  A  E  R  E  C  E  A  V  A  C  S
O  I  E  E  P  A  S  T  A  A  T  T  I  N  E
F  S  M  F  R  O  Z  E  E  D  E  R  U  A  S
```

BREAD	DIETS	NUTRITION	SOUP
BURGERS	FISH	PASTA	STARTERS
CEREALS	FOOD	READY MEALS	SWEETS
CHOCOLATE	FROZEN	RICE	VEGAN
DAIRY	FRUIT	SALAD	VEGETABLES
DESSERTS	MEAT	SAUCE	VEGETARIAN

✱ Two or more words in a phrase, like FINDERS KEEPERS, will usually be hidden
separately in the grid.

KRISS KROSS

See how quickly you can fit the listed words into the interlocking grid. The shaded squares will reveal a favorite dish.

4 LETTERS
ABLE
DIME
FAWN
FOND

5 LETTERS
BRINE
SNORT

6 LETTERS
AIRING
APLOMB
COUNTY
FAMOUS
FUTILE
MANGLE
MENIAL
UNKNOT

7 LETTERS
INKWELL
TUGBOAT

8 LETTERS
ALIGNING
CRAWLING
IRONWORK
TRANQUIL

11 LETTERS
CATACLYSMIC
DISCHARGING

190 ARROWORD

The arrows show the direction in which the answer to each clue should be placed. When complete, rearrange the letters in the shaded squares to spell out something to eat at Thanksgiving.

Huge numbers	▼	Chop (wood)	▼	Square or circle, e.g.	▼	Trousers cut above the knee	Dance party
▶				▼			▼
Separated grain from (corn)		Which person?	▶			Thin fog	
▶			Weaponry	▶		▼	
Small dwelling		Of the eye	▶				
▶			Major fuel company	▶			
Melancholy		Is at ease	▼	Capital of Texas	Small Inuit canoe		Parts of a dollar
Intoxicated	▶	▼			▼	Married woman	▼
▶				Reverential wonder	▶	▼	
Puts to some purpose	Remain at home (4,2)	▶					
▶				Rear of a ship	▶		
In disagree-ment with	Boa constrictors, vipers, etc.	▶					

WHODUNNIT?

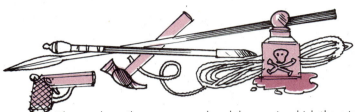

The murderer, the weapon used, and the area in which the crime was committed are all in the word lists but missing from the grid. Can you solve the mystery in the restaurant?

D	H	R	F	W	A	Y	O	E	E	R	C	O	R	K	S	C	R	E	T	R
X	A	O	F	I	S	S	F	W	N	E	L	E	T	O	H	D	C	C	E	T
T	R	H	I	N	W	I	N	U	T	G	S	G	U	E	S	L	A	D	M	S
K	W	Z	C	E	N	F	E	D	R	A	L	K	C	C	W	R	R	M	A	E
C	L	O	A	K	R	O	O	M	A	N	W	B	C	E	V	A	V	A	I	U
W	E	R	C	S	K	R	O	C	N	A	D	I	D	I	L	O	I	I	S	G
C	K	W	S	R	M	E	E	H	C	M	L	U	N	B	T	L	N	T	I	E
W	H	A	F	A	A	T	O	N	E	S	R	G	T	N	F	S	A	R	E	M
A	F	I	I	L	G	F	A	F	Y	T	M	A	G	N	U	S	P	A	R	R
Y	O	T	N	L	N	E	H	B	R	A	B	K	C	I	T	S	P	O	H	C
J	R	E	K	E	K	H	C	E	L	L	W	S	L	I	C	E	F	A	H	C
E	Q	I	W	C	S	C	G	P	Y	E	C	L	O	A	K	R	O	O	G	C
H	S	I	F	V	F	E	N	T	R	A	N	C	G	E	R	T	R	U	D	N

CHAD the CHEF
DINAH the DINER
GERTRUDE the GUEST
MAGNUS the MANAGER
MAISIE the MAITRE
    D'HOTEL
WAYNE the WAITER

CARVING KNIFE
CHINESE CHOPSTICKS
CORKSCREW
FISH SLICE
FORK
SKEWER

At the TABLE
CLOAKROOM
ENTRANCE
KITCHEN
LARDER
WINE CELLAR

✱ Only search for words that are in CAPITAL LETTERS. Two or more words in a phrase, like FINDERS KEEPERS, will usually be hidden separately in the grid.

192 **CODEWORD**

In this crossword, each letter of the alphabet appears as a code number. When you have replaced the decoded numbers with their letters in the grid, fill in the boxes at the bottom to reveal a saying or phrase.

	24	12	3	22	21	16	2		15	19	16	22
7		11		15		17		22		18		6
4	17	19	15	19		25	12	17	13	4	18	16
22				16		12		21		17		2
2	25	22	11	19	16	19		12	22	1	2	
26		11				16		18		22		8
16	4	11 L	12 O	21 G	3		10	22	15	18	16	18
2		12		15		20				19		22
	2	8	22	21		15	9	14	12	2	16	19
4		9		21		11		18				15
2	26	16	11	11	16	19		22	25	12	18	17
16		17		3		16		20		19		21
18	12	8	2		5	18	12	17	23	16	19	

A B C D E F G̷ H I J K L̷ M N Ø P Q R S T U V W X Y Z

1	2	3	4	5	6	7	8	9	10	11 L	12 O	13
14	15	16	17	18	19	20	21 G	22	23	24	25	26

THE SAYING OR PHRASE IS:

2	16	11	11		11	15	1	16

26	12	8	25	22	1	16	2

193 CROSSWORD

Rearrange the letters in the shaded squares to spell out a Tex-Mex dish.

ACROSS

3 Benchmark golf score (3)
7 Chinese tower temple (6)
8 Stretch (6)
9 Dot at the end of a sentence (4,4)
10 Mild-mannered (4)
11 Formal agreement (6)
12 Evaded (6)
15 Hamburger sauce (6)
18 Very short amount of time (6)
20 Imitated, copied (4)
22 Fragrant evergreen herb (8)
23 Surface for film projection (6)
24 Number in a cricket or soccer side (6)
25 Place for exercise (3)

DOWN

1 Large cat related to the leopard (6)
2 Variety of cabbage with a turnip-shaped stem (8)
3 Food cupboard (6)
4 Harvested (crops) (6)
5 Small particle of matter (4)
6 Sign of a cold (6)
11 Black, sticky material used on roads (3)
13 Long green salad vegetable (8)
14 Defective object (3)
16 Anticipate (6)
17 Paying for the use of (6)
18 Logical process (6)
19 Looked after in hospital (6)
21 Song for two (4)

1 What is crème Chantilly?

2 If the recipe states that fish should be cooked *en papillotte*, what does this mean?

3 The term "clafouti" is used to describe a pudding. How is it made?

4 Munchkin and Spooktacular are types of what?

5 What fruit is used in Melba sauce?

6 Basil is one of the most popular herbs today. It is used in a number of different dishes but with what salad fruit is it considered the ideal herb?

7 How do you prevent the mixture curdling when eggs are added to the creamed ingredients in a cake?

8 What is mageirocophobia?

Fit the pieces in the grid to spell out a pizza topping in each row.

ALMOND
CARAMEL
CHERRY
CHOCOLATES
CHOCOLATIER
COCOA
COCONUT
COFFEE
CREAM
DARK
DELICIOUS
FAVORITE
FUDGE
HAZELNUT
HONEY
LIQUEUR
LUXURY

MILK
NOUGAT
ORANGE
PEPPERMINT
PLAIN
PRALINE
RAISIN
RUM
SOFT CENTERS
STRAWBERRY
SUGAR
SWEETS
TOFFEE
TREAT
TURKISH DELIGHT
WHITE
WRAPPER

H	C	L	R	A	I	S	I	N	S	P
A	E	M	I	L	K	C	H	E	E	C
Z	N	F	B	Q	O	L	T	P	Y	H
E	T	E	U	C	U	A	P	P	R	E
L	E	R	O	N	L	E	A	N	U	R
N	R	C	I	O	R	E	U	D	X	R
U	S	A	C	M	C	A	G	R	U	Y
O	L	O	I	Y	H	R	G	D	L	T
P	H	N	L	R	O	U	E	U	U	L
C	T	Y	E	R	C	S	U	A	S	F
C	M	I	D	E	O	W	S	R	M	C
H	G	S	X	B	L	H	O	N	E	Y
E	T	I	H	W	A	I	R	N	R	T
R	Y	A	K	A	T	T	T	U	U	A
R	U	R	K	R	I	U	T	N	R	G
B	A	M	E	T	E	I	O	U	C	U
D	Z	A	M	S	R	C	D	S	O	O
E	E	T	I	R	O	V	A	F	C	N
S	L	P	O	C	E	E	E	F	F	O	C
Q	U	V	R	H	E	N	O	H	A	T
S	A	O	H	A	Z	E	L	N	U	T
T	W	W	I	A	L	P	F	R	N	E
R	D	E	L	C	A	I	K	F	G	O
E	A	F	E	L	I	I	N	N	O	J
A	R	F	M	T	S	L	A	E	T	T
T	R	O	A	H	S	R	E	V	F	I
G	N	T	R	S	O	F	U	D	O	H
D	W	R	A	P	P	E	R	W	S	W
E	F	I	C	T	H	G	I	L	E	D

✱ Two or more words in a phrase, like FINDERS KEEPERS, will usually be hidden separately in the grid.

See how quickly you can fit the listed words into the interlocking grid. The shaded squares will reveal the name of a vegetable.

4 LETTERS

FLAN
GRIT
MATE
PACT

5 LETTERS

HENNA
INAPT
MIXER
RUMBA

6 LETTERS

MARTYR
MORBID
PROFIT
SNORED
THRUST
TYRANT

7 LETTERS

FLATTER
REPAPER
THEOREM
THRIVED

8 LETTERS

ABRUPTLY
AVIATRIX
HIGH WIRE
VERBATIM

13 LETTERS

INTRINSICALLY
REVERENTIALLY

198 ARROWORD

The arrows show the direction in which the answer to each clue should be placed. When complete, rearrange the letters in the shaded squares to spell out a type of cracker.

	▼		▼		▼		▼
Express a desire		Sacred oaths		Fan-shaped edible shellfish		Set to go	
►							(shaded)
Woman who is no longer married		Lumberjack's chopping tool		Untidy writing		Consumes	
Bothered persistently	►		▼		(shaded)	▼	
Price charged for a service	Sentiment		Material used in pottery	►			
►	(shaded)		Decompose	►			Get-up-and-go
Confuse		Momentary slip	►				▼
►			__ Sampras, tennis great		(From) a distance	Skipjack or yellowfin, e.g.	
Measure of magnitude		Dinner dish	► ▼		▼	(shaded) ▼	
►		(shaded)		Soft animal hair	►		
Leg joint		Guitar-plucking noise	►				
►				Large skatelike fish	► (shaded)		

207

ARTICHOKE
AVGOLEMONO
AVOCADO
BAKLAVA
BALSAMIC
  VINEGAR
BOUILLABAISSE
CAPSICUM
CHORIZO
COURGETTE
CROUTONS
CRUDITES
DUCK CONFIT
EGG PLANT

FETA CHEESE
FOIE GRAS
FRENCH
GARLIC
GREEK
HALVA
HUMMUS
ITALIAN
LEMONS
LIME
MOUSSE
MOZZARELLA
OLIVES

ONION SOUP
OREGANO
PAELLA
PARMA HAM
PARMESAN
PASTA
PATE
PEPPERS
PESTO
PITA BREAD
PIZZA
RETSINA
SALAMI

SEAFOOD
SHERRY
SNAILS
SPAGHETTI
SPANISH
SUN-DRIED
  TOMATOES
TAPAS
TAPENADE
TARAMASALATA
TERRINE
TIRAMISU
TRUFFLES
WINE

✱ Two or more words in a phrase, like FINDERS KEEPERS, will usually be hidden
   separately in the grid.

```
A S E A F O O D O C P E D M T A P I S X T
A T P A E L L A O E A U C Z U E A N G I N
V E A S O U P U S I C I H H P C O V R F O
G S N L K F R S D M I R B P E T I A A N I
O S R F A G O R A M M R E U U E M S S O N
L U A O E S E I T O A E O O A I S P P C O
E O P T T B A P E Z S T R R S Z A E O A S
M M T A U U F M F Z L C I U E E Z L D E C
O E T S S P O B A A A H J F L G I I O H Y
N A I L A T I R R R B A K L A V A T P K C
I C Q E A E W T C E A E F S E P A N Q E D
O G L M N W T A I L A T I O O M A J O E E
L L R I B I S O C L T S G M O U S S S R I
H A W Z P O R R D A E R B T F O I B T G R
P S E L F F U R T U A R T I C H O K E A D
R G S U N D R I E N I T T E H G A P S R N
C R U D I T E S L T S F R E N C W E O L U
P E F T P H G A P L H P O M O U S S R I S
A E E I A A H A U A A P A N P E S T G F G
D H T L R G R A R B N B F G I Y D O O R T
T A E L M M D A T O E I A C H O R I Z O E
A A I F E A V A H N T R S I L E T R M F S
P C P S S L P A U O S Y G P S O T A E P C
R O A E A A S U M M U H F I S S T T A H C
L E M H N S R W M E E K R Z N O E N V R S
P A T A P A S I R L R S E Z E C I O U Z S
A E I S G E D Q S O E N N U V S H D H D A
R P P E I A T E O G T A C O H I I A U A L
M M N P C N V A R V S S H G M T X C M C A
L I B O E I E K P A I L I M E E K O M O M
V L V F L R S L I A N S X O M E L V U V I
J A M O B S S I A B A L L I U O B A Y A P
```

Fit the pieces in the grid to spell out a cuisine or cooking term in each row.

FOOD FACTS

- "Whiskey" is the international aviation word used to represent the letter "W."

- In *Forrest Gump*, Forrest's favorite soda is Dr Pepper.

- Avocados are poisonous to birds.

- Peanuts are not nuts; they are legumes.

- American mustard is milder than Dijon mustard.

- The vegetable fennel has an aniseed flavor.

- Chamomile is said to promote relaxation and sleep.

- When people accidently spill salt, they throw it over their left shoulder to represent throwing it into the devil's eyes.

WORD LADDER

Change one letter at a time (but not the position of any letter) to make a new word—and move from the word at the top of the box to the word at the bottom, using the exact number of rungs provided.

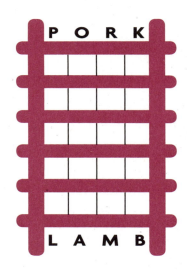

P O R K

L A M B

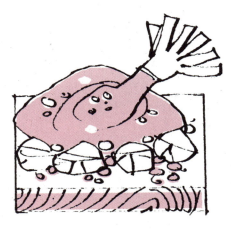

BOWL
BREAD
BRUNCH
COASTERS
CUTLERY
DISH
EVENING
  MEAL
FORKS
GLASSES
GUESTS
KNIVES
LADLE

LUNCH
NAPKINS
PLATES
PLATTER
REPAST
SALAD
SERVING
SOUP
SPOONS
SUPPER
TABLE
WATER JUG
WINE

B	R	U	N	C	H	F	C	P	F	S	H	H	T	U
P	K	T	W	W	N	O	L	G	E	Q	O	C	C	S
N	L	S	X	O	A	A	M	S	N	X	E	N	I	W
R	B	A	O	S	T	T	S	S	P	I	U	U	A	F
E	Q	P	T	T	I	A	E	E	S	L	V	L	O	O
P	S	E	I	T	L	D	G	R	A	E	A	R	M	R
A	R	R	E	G	E	U	S	P	L	T	K	T	E	P
S	C	U	T	L	E	R	Y	I	A	S	S	P	E	S
U	J	R	A	S	D	W	B	E	D	E	P	L	P	S
P	U	D	T	N	D	A	A	Y	H	U	O	W	I	Y
P	Z	S	H	I	U	V	L	T	S	G	O	O	W	I
E	U	S	G	K	N	I	V	E	E	B	N	B	D	K
A	I	O	S	P	G	L	A	S	S	Z	S	A	S	P
D	C	W	S	A	G	N	I	N	E	V	E	J	O	A
S	E	V	I	N	K	J	N	I	V	R	E	S	U	N
T	A	B	L	E	M	E	A	L	B	R	E	A	L	G

✳ Two or more words in a phrase, like FINDERS KEEPERS, will usually be hidden
  separately in the grid.

204 **KRISS KROSS**

See how quickly you can fit the listed words into the interlocking grid. The shaded squares will reveal the name of a shellfish.

3 LETTERS
APT

4 LETTERS
IDEA
IDLY
RAGE
SITE

5 LETTERS
AUDIO
EATEN
READY
RODEO
STYLE
USURP

6 LETTERS
ASSAIL
NAUSEA
NYLONS
STROLL

7 LETTERS
ADVISED
ASSAYED
GOODBYE
GRINNED
INSULAR
SPURTED

8 LETTERS
DUODENUM
TALLYING

12 LETTERS
DEMONSTRABLE
UNPLEASANTLY

205 ARROWORD

The arrows show the direction in which the answer to each clue should be placed. When complete, rearrange the letters in the shaded squares to spell out a type of cheese (8,4).

South Pacific island	▼	Run at a slow steady pace	▼	__ Winslet, *Titanic* actress	▼	Knox or Lauderdale, e.g.	▼
Fruit also known as an alligator pear ▶							
By way of		Of sound		Washtub		Begin to move	
▶		▼	Most excellent	▼		▼	
Large brass-band instrument ▶					Fugitive		Jupiter and Venus, e.g.
▶			Day out ▶		▼		▼
Auction offer	Short prayer before a meal		Throw, toss ▶				
Deity	▼ ▶		▼	Bob __, Mr. *Tambourine Man* singer		Thick string	
Covered shopping arcade		Desire strongly, feel longing ▶				▼	❦
▶				Sadness ▶			
Jockey's strap		Adjust, alter ▶					
▶				Word of consent ▶			

```
C A D Z U K D
H V E S U G A R
I I S P T B J V T
C T T I K B A E F F B S I A E B L B
K N R N O C L K B F R E N C H E D E
P E I T D O I A E L O E M E G L Y A
E L N S E E E H C D A D N U E E O N
C I G G K E R N C K U C M C N R S S
P M A N G E T O U T E E K D M P G B
G L S P I O P H X M S Y I E L I M A
F O Z N A B R A G T L K E P Y G P G
A Q S S A U Q R S K I D N E R E W U
T D A P N P S I T C T T S E E P D S
S C Z N R O B C U I N E E F F O C B
A N E U Y O P O O R E E G P Y H R S
O R O A K O U T R A L N A O C O C I
T D O P Z I T E P H U T E K A B N O
G A R B A N Z S S M S K I D N E R P
```

ADZUKI	COFFEE	KIDNEY	on TOAST	SEED
BAKED	FLAGEOLET	LEGUMES	PETIT POIS	SOY
BEANS	FRENCH	LENTIL	PINTO	SPROUTS
BLACK-EYED	GARBANZO	LIMA	POD	STRING
BROAD	GREEN	MANGETOUT	RED	SUGAR SNAP
CHICKPEA	HARICOT	MUNG	RUNNER	
COCOA				

✳ Only search for words that are in CAPITAL LETTERS. Two or more words in a phrase, like FINDERS KEEPERS, will usually be hidden separately in the grid.

In this crossword, each letter of the alphabet appears as a code number. When you have replaced the decoded numbers with their letters in the grid, fill in the boxes at the bottom to reveal a saying or phrase.

	22		14		10		2		26		20	
25	4	6	18		15	1	4		8	18	21	20
	10		18		26		20		26		26	
23	16	2	5	26	1		20	4	12	2	10	9
	19				6		19				2	
		24	16	15	10	12	26	2	2 **T**	26		
			5			4			4 **U**			
		4	23	20	26	2	2	16	1 **N**	15		
	24				1		16				3	
24	3	18	13	26	6		10	19	19	18	11	20
	18		16		16		12		18		5	
20	23	16	1		8	16	10		17	16	1	20
	20		6		26		20		2		20	

A B C D E F G H I J K L M N̸ O P Q R S̸ U̸ V W X Y Z

| 1 **N** | 2 **T** | 3 | 4 **U** | 5 | 6 | 7 | 8 | 9 | 10 | 11 | 12 | 13 |
| 14 | 15 | 16 | 17 | 18 | 19 | 20 | 21 | 22 | 23 | 24 | 25 | 26 |

THE SAYING OR PHRASE IS:

| 19 | 16 | 13 | 26 | | 23 | 26 | 10 | 20 | | 16 | 1 |

| 10 | | 23 | 18 | 6 |

208 CROSSWORD

Rearrange the letters in the shaded squares to spell out a type of pasta.

ACROSS

7 ___ shoots, vegetable used in Chinese meals (6)

8 Brown (food) with a little fat (3-3)

9 Two performers (3)

10 Keep out of view (4)

11 Fermented grape juice (4)

12 Every part (of) (3)

14 Military uniform color (5)

17 State west of Wyoming (5)

19 Lodge made from logs (5)

20 ___ Suzette, dessert pancake (5)

22 Nephew's sister (5)

24 Style of American theatrical dance (3)

26 Halt (4)

28 Earth-dwelling creature (4)

29 Illuminated (3)

30 Takings or wages (6)

31 Square or round drink sachet (3,3)

DOWN

1 Hot root plant, often eaten in salad (6)

2 In a position (to) (4)

3 Russian drink (5)

4 Ruin (5)

5 Was acquainted with (4)

6 Meal combining the early morning and midday ones (6)

13 Seventh zodiac sign (5)

15 Mature (3)

16 Freeze over (3)

17 *Holiday* ___, Bing Crosby film (3)

18 Woodcutting tool (3)

21 Light-sensitive part of the eye (6)

23 Breakfast grain (6)

24 Stories, legends (5)

25 Trivial (5)

27 Indoor game usually played with sixteen balls (4)

28 Frail, feeble (4)

1 How is a Spanish omelet served differently from the usual type?

2 The drink kirsch is made from which fruit?

3 In the U.S. we call it "broiling." What is it called in Britain?

4 When a dish is called *à la Lyonnaise*, what ingredient must it contain?

5 Oeufs à la Bourguignonne is a classic French dish. How are the eggs cooked?

6 What happens to shellfish if it is overcooked?

7 Calrose, Wehani, and jasmine are all types of what?

8 What meat is sometimes added to a Caesar salad?

210 **WORDWHEEL**

Using only the letters in the wordwheel, you have ten minutes to find as many words as possible, none of which may be plurals, foreign words, or proper nouns. Each word must be of three letters or more, all must contain the central letter, and letters can only be used once in every word. There is at least one nine-letter word in the wheel.

211 EGG HEAD

There are more EGGS than meet the eye here—how many can you find?

```
                    E  S  B  S
                 D  G  G  G  G  K  M  E
           K  S  G  Y  W  G  G  F  G  C  G  L
        E  G  S  X  X  E  E  H  S  G  G  E  G  E
     E  G  G  S  S  G  G  E  K  G  C  E  G  G  S  E
     E  Y  E  G  S  I  K  E  N  G  V  E  G  K  E  G
  V  A  V  V  G  S  M  A  G  S  E  S  S  G  G  G  G  R
  S  W  Q  G  E  G  M  W  G  W  G  A  J  G  G  G  S  O
  G  G  E  U  G  U  S  T  S  D  W  G  S  M  G  S  M  N
  E  G  G  S  G  S  G  G  E  X  G  Y  E  G  G  S  U  S
  S  G  G  E  S  E  G  G  S  E  E  S  G  G  E  E  C  F
  A  G  J  G  G  Z  X  F  G  G  G  P  R  Y  G  S  D  G
  I  L  G  G  U  B  N  I  G  G  G  G  J  G  P  G  O  O
  S  E  S  E  J  N  C  O  E  V  S  E  S  V  O  G  H  M
  B  Z  Y  L  Q  I  R  E  W  T  J  D  Q  X  A  E  Z  P
  S  G  G  E  E  E  F  B  E  L  S  E  G  G  S  S  I  E
  F  G  D  S  G  R  G  L  G  S  G  G  E  G  S  G  G  A
  Q  I  G  G  G  T  E  G  G  S  G  E  G  K  Z  G  E  T
  D  G  S  E  S  S  C  S  S  H  E  E  U  E  S  E  U  R
  E  Q  N  B  P  E  J  Z  R  H  H  E  X  T  O  P  E  Y
```

KRISS KROSS

See how quickly you can fit the listed words into the interlocking grid. The shaded squares will reveal the name of a variety of soup.

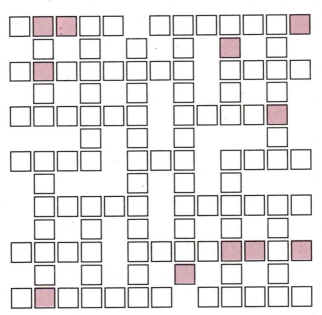

3 LETTERS
GIG

4 LETTERS
DIVA
FIRM
OBEY
TIDY

5 LETTERS
AHEAD
ALPHA
ASIDE
COCOA
INFER
NORTH
PSALM
SCOPE

6 LETTERS
ANNUAL
FATTEN

7 LETTERS
BRAZIER
EARTHED
JUNIPER
POULTRY
PRIMARY
TENUOUS

8 LETTERS
ACCUSTOM
HALLOWED

12 LETTERS
STENOGRAPHER
UNMANAGEABLE

The arrows show the direction in which the answer to each clue should be placed. When complete, rearrange the letters in the shaded squares to spell out an herb.

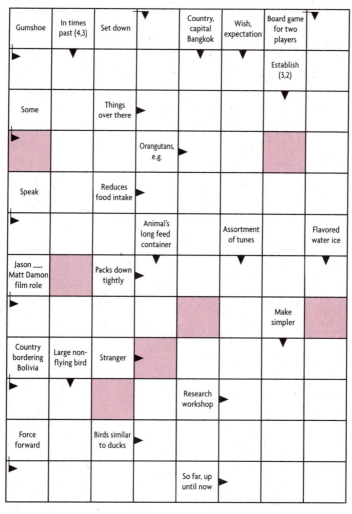

```
C R A S P B E R R Y P A W P A W
A N O M M I S R E P I H E S O R
N E N I R A T C E N A Y A P A P
T A V A U G R A P E F R U I T W
A B I N E Y R R E B E L K C U H
L M O H O N E Y D E W E S R Y Y
O B E Y T M I L N Q T T Y A R R
U E L D S S E T J A R R B N R R
P L L U L E R L N A R I K B E E
E P X O E A N A W E L U P E B B
Q P T G D B R B B B M B P R D N
U A A N A G E K E Q E E E R U A
I E U A E R C R U R A M L Y O G
N N Q M R A R A R C R O I C L O
C I O Y L Y T Z H Y K Y V L C L
E P L B G R O W A N B E R R Y M
```

BILBERRY
BLACKBERRY
BLUEBERRY
BOYSENBERRY
CANTALOUPE
CLEMENTINE
CLOUDBERRY
CRANBERRY
GRAPEFRUIT
GUAVA
HONEYDEW
HUCKLEBERRY
KUMQUAT
LEMON
LIME
LOGANBERRY
LOQUAT
MANGO
MEDLAR
NECTARINE
PAPAYA
PAWPAW
PEACH
PERSIMMON
PINEAPPLE
POMEGRANATE
QUINCE
RASPBERRY
ROSEHIP
ROWANBERRY
STRAWBERRY

In this crossword, each letter of the alphabet appears as a code number. When you have replaced the decoded numbers with their letters in the grid, fill in the boxes at the bottom to reveal a saying or phrase.

17	16	22	5	19	22	16	22		11	4	26	17
16		19		14		3		9		16		22
6	8	14	16	6		17	8	11	12	26	15	16
26		6		2		25		19		22		11
25	8	2	14		11	2	14	10	16	23	23	8
		13		10		7		10				9
9	8	14	24	25	7		26	25	11	2	1	16
26				26		18		16		22 **R**		
23	4	19	24	24	16	22	7		3	8 **I**	9	9
8		9		24		16		26		24 **G**		4
9	21	19	16	16	20	16		10	25	26	8	22
10		26		6		11		26		3		19
7	2	25	12		11	4	26	22	3	8	14	24

A B C D E F ~~G~~ H ~~I~~ J K L M N O P Q ~~R~~ S T U V W X Y Z

1	2	3	4	5	6	7	8 **I**	9	10	11	12	13
14	15	16	17	18	19	20	21	22 **R**	23	24 **G**	25	26

THE SAYING OR PHRASE IS:

9	3	16	25	25	9		10	8	9	4	7

216 **PATHFINDER**

Beginning with the D in the square box, follow a continuous path to find 17 fast-food chains. The trail passes through each and every letter once, and may twist up, down, or sideways, but never diagonally.

D	I	N	B	E	L	L	W	Z	E	L	A	P
O	M	O	O	R	K	Y	E	T	P	S	P	A
I	P	S	C	E	M	P	S	E	R	T	S	J
Z	W	E	A	T	E	R	I	T	N	U	H	O
Z	A	N	D	Y	S	K	E	Z	O	D	N	S
N	G	A	S	E	A	C	L	K	I	N	I	B
S	O	R	T	T	L	E	S	N	I	H	G	B
U	D	S	I	L	L	A	M	U	T	W	Y	O
D	D	R	I	S	D	N	C	D	E	C	T	L
S	C	I	V	N	S	O	D	G	N	A	S	E
P	O	N	E	I	K	E	R	K	I	Y	K	R
I	S	T	U	P	I	G	R	U	O	R	C	O
Z	Z	A	H	P	E	R	S	B	C	O	C	O

BIG BOY	LITTLE CAESARS	SONIC DRIVE-IN
BURGER KING	MCDONALD'S	TACO BELL
DOG N SUDS	PAPA JOHN'S	WENDY'S
DOMINO'S PIZZA	PIZZA HUT	WETZEL'S PRETZELS
DUNKIN' DONUTS	ROCKY ROCOCO	WHITE CASTLE
KRISPY KREME	SKIPPERS	

- Justin Timberlake sang the "I'm lovin' it" jingle for McDonald's.

- A cooked or hard-boiled egg will spin; an uncooked or soft-boiled one will not.

- The cereals in *The Simpsons* are called Krusty Flakes and Krusty-Os.

- Comice, Concord, Anjou, and Bartlett are all pear varieties.

- Barbecue cooking has many names around the world, including barbeque, Bar-B-Cue, Bar-B-Q, BBQ, barbi, barbique, and Cue and Q.

- Bands and singers with food or drink in their name include: Red Hot Chili Peppers, Meat Loaf, Salt n Pepa, Spice Girls, Hot Tuna, Vanilla Ice, Pearl Jam, Brandy, and Ice Cube.

- Song titles featuring food and drink:

"Candy Shop"	50 Cent
"One Bad Apple"	The Osmonds
"Candyman"	Christina Aguilera
"Popcorn Love"	New Edition
"Orange Crush"	REM
"Cornflake Girl"	Tori Amos
"Gin and Juice"	Snoop Dog
"Honey"	Mariah Carey
"The Onion Song"	Marvin Gaye
"Cherry Lips"	Garbage
"Milkshake"	Keli

218 CROSSWORD

Rearrange the letters in the shaded squares to spell out a type of snack food (6,5).

ACROSS

1 Clean (the floor) (3,2)
4 Individual pastry, often iced (7)
8 Fully booked event (4,3)
9 Supply (with) (5)
10 Circular pyramid (4)
11 Small house or shelter (3)
12 Brief note (4)
15 ___ butter, popular spread (6)
16 Ice cream with syrup and toppings (6)
19 Chat, gossip (4)
21 Chinese frying pan (3)
22 Action word (4)
26 Iron or copper (5)
27 Inability to remember (7)
28 Seed sometimes used in rye bread and sauerkraut (7)
29 Wide, round, open dish (5)

DOWN

1 Notes played by an orchestra (5)
2 Cooked dish of cornmeal and water (7)
3 Lacking wealth (4)
4 Fruits such as limes and oranges (6)
5 Flans (4)
6 Keenly perceptive, sharp (5)
7 Search new territory (7)
13 Billiard rod (3)
14 Make a purchase of (3)
15 Washington, D.C.'s river (7)
17 Garments for girls (7)
18 Plant science (6)
20 In the future (5)
23 Intellect (5)
24 Behind in time (4)
25 Arrogantly superior person (4)

219 **COCKTAILS**

Try one of these cocktails!

```
      C  O  L  L  I  N  S  M  O  P  E  R  A  A  E  G
      M  A  R  T  I  N  I  A  R  D  T  D  D  L  W  P
      M  I  N  T  K  K  R  U  R  H  A  A  H  E
      G  N  I  L  S  S  G  O  Y  I  Y  I  L  X
      A  G  O  T  A  R  A  S  Q  O  S  U  R  R
      R  E  G  O  R  R  U  R  K  J  D  N
      B  O  N  A  C  I  R  E  M  A  A  I
      E  L  S  I  R  T  Y  D  L  T  Y  M
      R  A  I  A  A  F  N  T  G  D
      I  O  C  T  M  D  A  R  I  A
      R  U  P  K  A  H  X  E  M  L
      U  I  A  N  N  E  G  L
      R  S  A  G  T  L  N  E
      Y  M  S  I  N  A  I  T
         D  H  I  T  I  T
         W  O  J  A  A  S
         Y  M  O  O  N  M
            O  L  L  A
            T  L  R  B
               Y  B
```

ALEXANDER
AMERICANO
BLACK
   RUSSIAN
BLOODY MARY
DAIQUIRI
DRY MARTINI
GIMLET
JOLLY ROGER
KIR ROYALE
MAI TAI
MANHATTAN
MARGARITA
MINT JULEP
OPERA
ROSITA
SARATOGA
SINGAPORE SLING
STINGER
TOM COLLINS
WHISKEY SOUR
WHITE LADY

✳ Two or more words in a phrase, like FINDERS KEEPERS, will usually be hidden
  separately in the grid.

220 **KRISS KROSS**

See how quickly you can fit the listed words into the interlocking grid. The shaded squares will reveal the name of a drink.

3 LETTERS
FAN
LET

4 LETTERS
COLD
QUIT

5 LETTERS
CLUMP
GRIND
IDEAL
SITAR

6 LETTERS
ANTLER
ELUDED
HEALED
MAINLY
RUNNER
SKYLAB

7 LETTERS
ASEPTIC
TRADERS

8 LETTERS
PARALLEL
UNSEEING

9 LETTERS
CONCEIVED
DEPENDENT
PERMANENT

13 LETTERS
HYDROELECTRIC
INEFFECTIVELY

221 **WORD LADDER**

Change one letter at a time (but not the position of any letter) to make a new word—and move from the word at the top of the box to the word at the bottom, using the exact number of rungs provided.

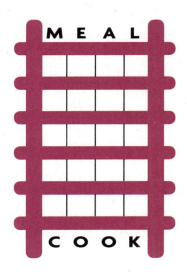

M E A L

C O O K

SOLUTIONS

PUZZLE 1

Dessert: APPLE CRISP

PUZZLE 3

Type of grape: MERLOT

PUZZLE 4

CRUSH, SUN DROP, NEHI, SHASTA, SUNKIST, CRYSTAL
LIGHT, COUNTRY TIME, SLICE, BIG RED, SCHWEPPES,
ORANGINA, MOXIE, SEVEN UP, PEPSI, COCA-COLA,
YOO HOO, DR PEPPER, FAYGO, DIET RITE, HAWAIIAN
PUNCH, MOUNTAIN DEW, SQUIRT, SNAPPLE

PUZZLE 5

American as apple pie

PUZZLE 7

Type of wine: CHARDONNAY

PUZZLE 8

1. Union Oyster House.
2. Prawns.
3. A squash.
4. Almonds.
5. Butter, eggs, and sugar.
6. Bran provides essential fiber.
   It comes from the inner husks of
   wheat, oats, and other grains.
7. Beet.
8. 76.

SOLUTIONS

PUZZLE 9

```
A D E Q U A T E . J E S T
X . X . G . A . F . V . E
I . M P E L . T R O P I C S
N . L . Y . T . R . C . T
G R O G . C O N F E T T I
. I . W . O . E . . . F
D U T I E S . P I G S T Y
U . . B . V . T . T . .
R O A D S H O W . Z I N C
A . M . I . O . A . M . L
B O A S T E D . S A U N A
L . Z . E . O . K . L . N
E Y E D . B O O S T I N G
```

A chip on the shoulder

PUZZLE 10

```
. G . R . . . S
V I G I L A N T
. R . M A D . R
F L Y . Z O N E
. F . V I R U S
D R Y . N E T S
. I . . G . S
. E S P . F . R
O N P A R A D E
. D E S I R E S
. . A . S E N T
H A R V E S T S
```

Brand of beer: MILLER

PUZZLE 12

M	T	D	C	B	P	C
A	O	A	E	A	O	H
R	M	M	L	N	T	E
R	A	S	E	A	A	R
O	T	O	R	N	T	R
W	O	N	Y	A	O	Y

PUZZLE 13

The words in the correct order are:
sTock, pestO, gRape, Tart, scampI, bowL,
fLavor, meAt.
The item of food is TORTILLA.

PUZZLE 15

```
S . C . L . H . F . F . R
C O R R O D E . A L I B I
A . I . U . R . I . J . S
L E M O N . B U R R I T O
D . I . G . . E . . . T
. U N D E R C U R R E N T
S . A . . A . . P . O
W A L K I E T A L K I E
I . . G . . A . D . B
M A T I N E E . W H E E L
M . I . I . A . M . M . I
E L E C T . S T A T I O N
R . D . E . Y . N . C . D
```

Breakfast food: YOGURT

PUZZLE 17

```
F A I T H F U L N E S S
I . N . O . N . A . W . P
F O C U S . T A S T I E R
E . E . T . I . T . N . A
. U N W A V E R I N G L Y
S . S . . D . L . . . I
T H E S I S . H Y P H E N
A . . M . P . . A . G
M U L T I T A S K I N G
I . A . T . R . N . D . E
N I T R A T E . O I L E D
A . H . T . N . L . E . G
. R E L E N T L E S S L Y
```

Spice: CINNAMON

PUZZLE 18

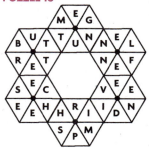

SOLUTIONS

PUZZLE 19

Tilda at the till, string bag, entrance

PUZZLE 20

Cry over spilt milk

PUZZLE 21

Chicken dish: BUFFALO WINGS

PUZZLE 22

1. Add one or more diced potatoes and simmer in the liquid for a short time, then remove: They absorb much of the salt. If a suitable dish, add milk or cream, which lessens the salty taste.
2. Smoked cod's roe.
3. Lasagne.
4. Cheese.
5. Yes.
6. Ladies' fingers, gumbo, and bhindi.
7. Both—most trout are freshwater but salmon trout is a saltwater fish.
8. Hickory nuts.

PUZZLE 23

1. Carrot 2. Potato 3. Lettuce 4. Pea
5. Leek 6. Kale 7. Onion 8. Celery
9. Radish 10. Beet

PUZZLE 25

Dessert sauce: CUSTARD

PUZZLE 26

Tex-Mex food: FAJITAS

PUZZLE 28

ICING ON THE CAKE

SOLUTIONS

PUZZLE 30

Vegetable: SPINACH

PUZZLE 32

Tangy ingredient: LEMON PEEL

PUZZLE 33

On toast: JELLY

PUZZLE 35

A pinch of salt

PUZZLE 36

Dairy product: CREAM CHEESE

PUZZLE 37

1. Cutting into it with a sharp knife, to give the effect of layers—which helps to make the pastry rise.
2. Insert a sharp knife where the leg joins the body. If the juices run pink, the bird is NOT cooked. Juices should be clear.
3. (a) 28.35 grams. (b) 453.60 grams.
4. Chocolate.
5. Add a few drops of vinegar to the water and swirl briskly before adding the egg.
6. The beard.
7. Metal is a better conductor of heat than ceramic or glassware.
8. The dish is topped with sugar, which is heated so it becomes crisp and brown.

SOLUTIONS

PUZZLE 38

1. Potato 2. Leek 3. Cauliflower
4. Spinach 5. Eggplant 6. Cabbage
7. Lettuce 8. Broccoli 9. Turnip 10. Sprout
11. Sweetcorn 12. Carrot 13. Corn
The other name for the avocado is:
ALLIGATOR PEAR.

PUZZLE 40

S		D		U		O		R		S		A
T	H	I	N	N	E	D		O	F	T	E	N
A		S		B		D		C		O		T
M	A	C	H	O		S	C	O	R	P	I	O
P		O		R				C				N
	P	U	G	N	A	C	I	O	U	S	L	Y
R		N				U				P		M
I	N	T	O	L	E	R	A	N	T	L	Y	
N				A				A		E		A
S	W	A	M	P	E	D		C	A	N	A	L
I		L		E		U		H		D		I
N	A	S	A	L		P	R	O	V	I	N	G
G		O		S		E		S		D		N

Dessert: APPLE PIE

PUZZLE 41

Snack food: GOLDFISH

PUZZLE 43

CUT THE MUSTARD

PUZZLE 44

The nine-letter word is MILKSHAKE.

PUZZLE 46

1. Ginger 2. Paprika
3. Rosemary 4. Parsley
5. Vanilla 6. Cloves
The tastebud teaser is Garlic.

PUZZLE 48

M	A	Y	O	R		A	T	T	E	M	P	T
	L		R		G		H		X		L	
C	O	N	C	E	R	T	O		I	C	E	D
	H		H		A		U		L		A	
V	A	C	A	N	T		S	W	E	E	T	
		R		I		A			E			
U	S	E	D		F	I	N		C	O	D	E
	O			Y		D		H				
	R	A	B	B	I		F	L	A	G	O	N
	C		O		N		O		N		L	
R	E	I	N		G	A	L	A	C	T	I	C
	R		G		L		D		E		V	
S	Y	N	O	N	Y	M		A	D	D	E	D

Thick syrup: MOLASSES

PUZZLE 49

		Z			P		
D	E	F	E	R	R	A	L
	V		B	E	E		E
N	E	B	R	A	S	K	A
	R		A	L	I	A	S
R	Y	E		D	Y	E	
		G	L	E	E		
I	O	W	A		N		I
	N		S	A	T	I	N
J	A	V	E	L	I	N	S
	I		S	P	A	T	E
A	R	K		S	L	O	T

Type of grape: ZINFANDEL

PUZZLE 51

1. Relish 2. Garlic 3. Pepper
4. Nutmeg 5. Pickle 6. Ginger

SOLUTIONS

PUZZLE 52

Accompaniment: DUMPLINGS

PUZZLE 53

1. (a) The fish breaks and loses taste and texture. (b) It becomes very hard and "leathery."
2. A thousand layers; also the name of the French pastry.
3. Duff.
4. Lettuce.
5. Basil and pine nuts.
6. Skin the tomatoes, halve them and remove the seeds, then dice the pulp.
7. Short, moderately thick tubes.
8. Scrambled egg.

PUZZLE 54

BEEF, BEER, DEER, DEEM, SEEM, STEM, STEW

PUZZLE 56

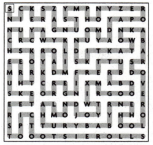

SNICKERS, ZAGNUT, SYMPHONY, ZERO, PAYDAY, MOUNDS, KIT KAT, WONKA BARS, DOVE, ROLO, OH HENRY!, BABY RUTH, ALMOND JOY, TWIX, MR. GOODBAR, BUTTERFINGER, ROCKY ROAD, MILKY WAY, CRUNCH, SKOR, THREE MUSKETEERS, TOPIC, TOOTSIE ROLLS

PUZZLE 57

Type of cheese: COLBY

PUZZLE 59

BUY A LEMON

SOLUTIONS

PUZZLE 60

The nine-letter word is SHORTCAKE.

PUZZLE 62

Brand of beer: MICHELOB

PUZZLE 63

Mystery lady: Sarah Michelle Gellar

PUZZLE 64

Pastry ingredient: SHORTENING

PUZZLE 65

Drink: CIDER

PUZZLE 67

UPSET THE APPLECART

PUZZLE 68

Fruit: TANGERINE

SOLUTIONS

PUZZLE 69

1. Thin (minute) slices from sirloin, rib, or rump.
2. A little sugar plus cornstarch.
3. Because they were thought to be an aphrodisiac.
4. Spinach.
5. Pavlova.
6. Nutmeg is the seed of the nutmeg tree; mace is the dried outer coating of the nutmeg.
7. Albumen.
8. Cooked ground meat, flavored with spices and dried fruit.

PUZZLE 70

Wine, Pear, Meal, Eat, Fig, Plate, Pork, Tuna, Fish, Water, Salt, Chip, Pecan, Beef, Gin

PUZZLE 71

Moderation in all things

PUZZLE 72

Stew: CASSEROLE

PUZZLE 73

Sauce dip: SALSA

PUZZLE 75

VARIETY IS THE SPICE OF LIFE

PUZZLE 76

POPCORN LOVE, AMERICAN PIE, THE ONION SONG, STRAWBERRY FIELDS FOREVER, MASHED POTATO, ANIMAL CRACKERS, LITTLE GREEN APPLES, CORNFLAKE GIRL, ONE BAD APPLE, MAYONNAISE, CRUISING FOR BURGERS, THE PINA COLADA SONG

SOLUTIONS

PUZZLE 78

A	D	S			D	W	S				
C	U	R	L	I	E	R		R	O	A	S	T
A		A		M	A	I		I			U
D	E	W		M	O	T	I	V	A	T	E	D
E			E		A		E	R
M	A	J	O	R		T	O	R	R	E	N	T
I		U			O			S			E
C	A	R	I	B	O	U		B	A	S	I	S
		A		A		I		R			T
A	U	S	T	R	A	L	I	A		D	O	C
R		S		L		L		N		I		A
M	A	I	Z	E		E	N	D	L	E	S	S
Y		C		Y		Y			T		E

Ice cream flavor: VANILLA

PUZZLE 80

U		S		P			J		P		J
P	A	Y	S	L	I	P		A	Z	U	R	E
L		M		A		A		I		M		W
I	M	P	L	Y		R	E	L	E	A	S	E
F		T			A		B					L
T	O	O		A	T	T	A	I	N	E	D
S		M		M		R		R		L		P
	A	S	T	E	R	O	I	D		E	K	E
Q			N		O			V				R
U	N	C	L	A	S	P		P	E	A	C	H
I		I		B		E		A		T		A
E	X	T	O	L		R	E	G	R	O	U	P
T		E		E			E		R			S

A piece of cake

PUZZLE 81

		C		F		P
P	E	S	O		A	I	R
	Q		C	O	N		E
D	U	C	K		M	A	T
	A		T	R	A	C	E
P	L	E	A		I	N	N
		I	D	L	E	D
B	A	I	L				S
	L		B	A	T	S
D	I	C	A	P	R	I	O
	B		R	E	I	G	N
K	I	D		D	O	N	E

Breakfast item: PANCAKES

PUZZLE 83

Chowder, Broth, Spoon, Menudo, Tomato, Gumbo, Tureen; spelling Crouton.

PUZZLE 84

	W	O	S	C		F	U
C	I	A	B	A	T	T	A		L	I	N	E
	T		L		E	N		A			P
S	H	R	I	M	P		A	N	G	E	L
	I		V		U		P			U
A	N	T	I		P	E	E	L	I	N	G	S
		O				N
S	C	H	N	A	P	P	S		V	E	S	T
	A			A		T		I		Q
	R	U	L	E	R		O	U	T	P	U	T
	R		A		A		R		I		A
C	O	R	K		D	I	M	I	N	I	S	H
	T		E		E		Y		G		H

Tex-Mex dish: CHILI CON CARNE

PUZZLE 85

1. Spinach.
2. Dust the moist fish with seasoned flour first.
3. Avocado.
4. Protein.
5. Australian cakes made with squares of sponge, coated with chocolate icing, then rolled in desiccated coconut.
6. The canned fish is generally brisling or ultra-small sardines.
7. Saffron, which comes from a special crocus.
8. Shaken, not stirred.

PUZZLE 86

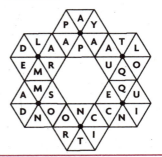

SOLUTIONS

PUZZLE 88

Cake topping: FROSTING

PUZZLE 89

FLAN, FLAT, FEAT, PEAT, PERT, PART, TART

PUZZLE 91

DON'T PUT ALL YOUR EGGS IN ONE BASKET

PUZZLE 92

"When we lose twenty pounds . . . we may be losing the twenty best pounds we have. We may be losing the pounds that contain our genius, our humanity, our love and honesty."

PUZZLE 94

Salad dressing: MAYONNAISE

PUZZLE 96

Name of broth: BOUILLON

PUZZLE 97

On a burger: RELISH

SOLUTIONS

PUZZLE 99

THE BEST THING SINCE SLICED BREAD

PUZZLE 100

Fast food: HAMBURGER

PUZZLE 101

1. Burger King.
2. Jerky.
3. Stand it in a receptacle of water.
4. Oatmeal.
5. For cutting wafer-thin slices of potatoes, etc.
6. Quiche.
7. The large number of egg whites.
8. Soybeans.

PUZZLE 102

The letter pairs are PO, TA and TO, spelling POTATO.

PUZZLE 104

Hidden word: BREAD

PUZZLE 105

Cereal: CHEERIOS

PUZZLE 107

IN A NUTSHELL

SOLUTIONS

PUZZLE 109

CAP'N CRUNCH, QUISP, ALPHA-BITS, FRUITY PEBBLES, ZUCARITAS, SPECIAL K, COCOA KRISPIES, CORN FLAKES, FROOT LOOPS, LUCKY CHARMS, APPLE JACKS, CORN POPS, RAISIN BRAN, KING VITAMAN, HONEY SMACKS, GOLDEN CRISP, LIFE CEREAL

PUZZLE 111

The nine-letter word is SPAGHETTI.

PUZZLE 112

Brand of beer: COORS

PUZZLE 114

USE YOUR LOAF

PUZZLE 115

Wine-growing state: CALIFORNIA

PUZZLE 116

1. Orange rind means all the peel; zest is the top orange part free from pith.
2. A mixture of equal amounts of butter and flour.
3. Demerara.
4. Chocolate sauce.
5. The pea.
6. Scrambled—accounting for 20% of all eggs eaten.
7. Handle the crab: it should feel heavy for its size. If light, it is watery.
8. Virgin olive oil.

SOLUTIONS

PUZZLE 117

B	G	K	W	C	M	S
R	R	I	H	O	E	H
A	A	R	I	G	S	E
N	P	S	S	N	C	R
D	P	C	K	A	A	R
Y	A	H	Y	C	L	Y

PUZZLE 119

	B	E	A	D	I	N	G		U	S	E	D
P		L		I		O			T		A	
R	E	F	U	S	E	D		I	N	A	P	T
E		I		T		D		N		B		A
M	I	N	E	R		E	V	E	N	L	Y	
I			I		D		S		E		E	
S	C	R	I	B	E		S	T	O	D	G	Y
E		E		U		E		I			E	
	A	B	A	T	E	D		M	I	N	U	S
S		U		O		I		A		Y		O
P	O	K	E	R		T	A	B	U	L	A	R
E		E			E		L		O		E	
W	A	D	E		E	D	D	Y	I	N	G	

Vegetable: ONIONS

PUZZLE 120

	B		I				M
F	A	N	T	A	S	I	A
	L		S	P	A		K
S	L	Y		R	U	L	E
	E		D	I	C	E	D
C	R	Y		L	E	N	O
	I		A			D	
	N	I	G	H	T		S
J	A	D	E		R	A	W
		I	N	T	U	N	E
W	O	O	D		C	O	P
		T	A	L	E	N	T

Fruit for sauce: CRANBERRY

PUZZLE 122

P		S		P		G		G		A		E
E	P	O	C	H		O	I	L	S	K	I	N
E		L		O		V		O		I		D
L	O	V	A	B	L	E		B	A	N	J	O
S		E		I		R		E				W
	U	N	V	A	R	N	I	S	H	E	D	
	T								N			
	E	S	S	E	N	T	I	A	L	L	Y	
F			I		H		C		A		A	
A	D	O	P	T		E	X	T	O	R	T	S
L		P		H		M		U		G		I
S	Q	U	E	E	Z	E		A	H	E	A	D
E		S		R		S		L		D		E

EAT HUMBLE PIE

PUZZLE 123

RIND, RAND, RAID, SAID, SKID, SKIM, SKIN

PUZZLE 125

	O	F	T	E	N		K	I	S	S	E	D
O		U		A		C		N		W		E
B	A	N	D	S	T	A	N	D		E	W	E
A		G		T		U		E		A		R
M	A	I	N	E		L	U	X	U	R	Y	
A				R		I				I		
	M	A	G	N	I	F	I	C	E	N	T	
	P				L		H				A	
	T	O	M	A	T	O		I	D	E	A	L
S		L		N		W		A		M		I
P	R	O		G	R	E	E	N	G	A	G	E
U		G		L		R		T		I		N
R	H	Y	M	E	D		B	I	B	L	E	

Breakfast food: FRIED EGGS

SOLUTIONS

PUZZLE 127

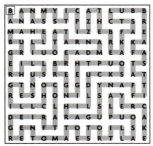

BANANAS, MYSTIC PIZZA, THE BREAKFAST CLUB, BREAKFAST AT TIFFANY'S, SUGARHILL, DUCK SOUP, THE GINGERBREAD MAN, RATATOUILLE, HAMBURGER HILL, SUNSET GRILL, CHOCOLAT, FRIED GREEN TOMATOES, TORTILLA SOUP, LAYER CAKE

PUZZLE 128

Eggs: SCRAMBLED

PUZZLE 130

SOUR GRAPES

PUZZLE 131

Fruit: WATERMELON

PUZZLE 132

1. To bake it without a filling.
2. The Netherlands.
3. The chicken.
4. Either.
5. Boar's Nest.
6. The chicken. Genesis 1:20: "fowl that may fly about the earth."
7. Either is correct; it is a matter of personal choice.
8. It is made from the root of maranta and it is mainly used to thicken liquid for clear glaze.

PUZZLE 133

1. Fig 2. Plum 3. Cherry 4. Banana
5. Kumquat

PUZZLE 135

COUCH POTATO

SOLUTIONS

PUZZLE 136

Spice: CUMIN

PUZZLE 138

1. Grapes **2.** Cherry **3.** Orange
4. Pawpaw **5.** Banana **6.** Squash

PUZZLE 139

The nine-letter word is SPEARMINT.

PUZZLE 141

Dessert: KEY LIME PIE

PUZZLE 143

Salad: COLESLAW

PUZZLE 144

Fruit: ORANGE

PUZZLE 146

BITE OFF MORE THAN YOU CAN CHEW

PUZZLE 147

Cocktail: PINA COLADA

SOLUTIONS

PUZZLE 148

1. The Chinese, in honor of spring.
2. These fish are rich in fish oils and omega 3—particularly important for good health and prevention of heart disease.
3. Crushed black or other colored peppercorns.
4. Parmesan cheese.
5. Tequila.
6. They should be halved and seeded, then grilled or baked until the skins turn black. They should then be placed in a plastic bag until cold.
7. Tortilla.
8. Vitamin C.

PUZZLE 149

C	O	P	T	S	O	G
H	N	E	O	A	L	A
E	I	P	M	L	I	R
E	O	P	A	A	V	L
S	N	E	T	M	E	I
E	S	R	O	I	S	C

PUZZLE 151

	S	P	I	C	E		K	N	E	E	L	
S		O		O			O		L		F
T	R	U	A	N	T		E	N	T	A	I	L
A		T		S	H		C		P		A
T	R	E	A	C	H	E	R	O	U	S	L	Y
E		D		I		A		N		E		S
		H	O	R	R	I	F	Y		
S		I		U		T		O		A		C
H	E	M	I	S	P	H	E	R	I	C	A	L
A		M		N		S		M		C		O
M	A	U	L	E	D		M	I	N	U	E	T
E		N		S			S		S		H
	T	E	R	S	E		S	T	E	E	R	

Seafood dish: SHRIMPS

PUZZLE 152

The nine-letter word is FRICASSEE.

PUZZLE 154

APPLE OF MY EYE

PUZZLE 155

Alex, Ashley, French, Vacation
Les, Sam, Indian, Office
Pat, Jo, Thai, Gym

PUZZLE 157

	M		A		S		P		L		P	
N	U	G	G	E	T		H	O	A	R	S	E
	S		A		A		O		W		Y	
P	E	A	R		R	O	B		N	I	C	E
	U		E		E		I			H	
S	M	I	L	E	D		A	N	C	H	O	R
	I		E				U	
S	T	R	E	S	S		H	O	T	D	O	G
	U		H		A			U	
C	R	A	B		A	I	R		P	A	T	H
	K		R		K		L		E		S	
S	E	S	A	M	E		E	N	A	M	E	L
	Y		N		R		M		K		T	

Salad vegetable: CELERY

SOLUTIONS

PUZZLE 159

Q	U	A	S	H	E	D		E	D		I	C	T
	N		I		A		V		E		O		
D	E	B	T	O	R		E	N	T	O	M	B	
	A		U		N		N		E		M		
E	S	S	A	Y		S	T	A	R	L	I	T	
	E		T		C		U				T		
		D	E	V	O	U	R	I	N	G			
	D			U		E		E		C			
C	U	L	L	I	N	G		W	I	D	O	W	
	C		A		T		D		G		R		
S	K	A	T	E	R		A	C	H	I	N	G	
	E		E		Y		D		E		E		
A	D	O	R	N		C	O	R	D	I	A	L	

Spice: GINGER

PUZZLE 160

	G		R		R		
M	A	Y	O		E	G	O
	L		C	O	G		P
S	E	E	K		A	T	E
		C	O	L	O	N	
I	D	O	L		E	N	D
	I		N	D	I	A	
S	P	A	M			Y	
	L		B	E	A	R	
C	O	M	E	D	I	A	N
	M		R	I	D	G	E
F	A	T		T	E	S	T

Type of grape: PINOT NOIR

PUZZLE 162

	R		S		F	E	Z		H		F	
T	A	T	T	O	O		E	X	O	D	U	S
	V		R		R		R		S		N	
S	I	L	E	N	T		O	U	T	C	R	Y
	N		E		U		T		E		U	
T	E	N	P	I	N	B	O	W	L	I	N	G
O			E		L				E			
W	A	T	E	R	C	H	E	S	T	N	U	T
	D		L		O		R		I		N	
M	O	J	I	T	O		A	C	C	U	S	E
	R		X		K		N		K		U	
G	E	M	I	N	I		C	H	E	R	R	Y
	D		R		E	Y	E		T		E	

Grape: CABERNET SAUVIGNON

PUZZLE 163

1. Cornflour.
2. Poached.
3. Clarified butter.
4. Small shaped pieces of puff pastry, used for garnish.
5. Tomato.
6. First soften it in a little cold liquid, then dissolve in a hot liquid.
7. African dried meat.
8. Arborio or any other medium-grain risotto rice.

PUZZLE 164

P	R	E	J	U	D	G	E		I	R	O	N
	E		A		O		A		N		P	
C	L	E	R	I	C		R	E	F	L	E	X
	I				T				L		N	
N	E	W	S	R	O	O	M		U	G	L	Y
	F		W		R		I		E		Y	
		D	E	T	A	I	L	I	N	G		
	Q		A		T		L		Z		A	
T	U	F	T		E	Y	E	P	A	T	C	H
	O		B			N					T	
A	T	T	A	C	H		N	A	P	K	I	N
	E		N		A		I		I		N	
U	S	E	D		S	C	A	V	E	N	G	E

GRAVY TRAIN

PUZZLE 166

D	E	L	V	I	N	G		A	D	A	P	T
	Y		E		U		P		O		A	
R	E	A	R	E	D		O	O	Z	I	N	G
	I		A		E		U		E		E	
I	N	A	N	E		B	L	U	N	T	L	Y
	G		D		O		T				S	
		P	A	N	D	E	R	I	N	G		
	H			D		Y		E		P		
S	U	C	K	I	N	G		S	T	R	A	P
	N		I		E		A		T		E	
S	T	Y	L	U	S		S	O	L	E	L	Y
	E		L		S		T		E		L	
G	R	A	S	S		W	I	L	D	C	A	T

Sandwich: PO BOYS

SOLUTIONS

PUZZLE 167

Dessert: CHEESECAKE

PUZZLE 169

1. CRAB
2. PASTA
3. BANANA
4. SALAD
5. ALFALFA
6. PAPAYA

PUZZLE 171

BEER, BEET, BENT, WENT, WANT, WANE, WINE

PUZZLE 173

C	O	M	M	U	N	I	C	A	T	E	D
A		O		M		N		W		M	A
P	L	U	M	B		R	E	F	R	A	I	N
E		R		R		O		U		I	O
	U	N	P	A	R	A	L	L	E	L	E	D
G		E				D		L			Y
I	N	D	O	O	R		P	Y	T	H	O	N
M			R		A			A			E
M	A	R	R	I	A	G	E	A	B	L	E
I		I		G		E		L		V		T
C	A	P	T	A	I	N		I	C	I	E	R
K		E		M		D		B		N	A
	I	R	R	I	T	A	T	I	N	G	L	Y

Fairground food: COTTON CANDY

PUZZLE 174

Breakfast dish: HASH BROWNS

PUZZLE 176

FLASH IN THE PAN

PUZZLE 177

Pizza topping: PEPPERONI

SOLUTIONS

PUZZLE 178

1. Strawberry.
2. Skate.
3. Sausages.
4. Central Perk.
5. They are an herb with a delicate onion taste.
6. It is not a wheat at all but an herb.
7. Cut small rounds or squares of thick bread. Neatly hollow out the centers (making flan shapes). Bake or deep fry until crisp. Fill with savory or sweet ingredients.
8. Chopped cooked bacon and grated cheese, preferably Gruyère.

PUZZLE 179

One answer is:
MEAT, HEAT, HEAD, DEAD, DEAF, LEAF, LOAF

PUZZLE 181

SOYBEAN, PUMPKIN, JALAPENO, RED KALE, APRICOT, ZUCCHINI, MANGO, TOMATO, CARROT, APPLE, POTATO, NECTARINE, LETTUCE, WATERMELON, PRICKLY PEAR, ASPARAGUS, CANTALOUPE, SQUASH, PEACH, BELL PEPPER, SWEET CORN, ONION, CHERRY

PUZZLE 182

Vegetable: MUSHROOM

PUZZLE 184

BRING HOME THE BACON

PUZZLE 185

The nine-letter word is CHAMPAGNE.

SOLUTIONS

PUZZLE 187

	P		S		F		T		B		A	
P	I	C	K	L	E		E	R	R	A	N	D
	L		I		T		E		E		G	
E	L	E	P	H	A	N	T		W	E	E	K
	A		J				O				R	
A	R	E	A		A	S	T	O	N	I	S	H
			C		R		A		O			
M	A	C	K	E	R	E	L		T	I	M	E
	L		E						E		A	
E	M	I	T		S	O	F	T	B	A	L	L
	O		U		T		A		O		T	
E	N	T	R	E	E		M	O	O	R	E	D
	D		N		D		E		K		D	

Type of sauce: BARBECUE

PUZZLE 189

	T		D		M		F		C		S	
F	U	T	I	L	E		A	I	R	I	N	G
	G		M		N		M		A		O	
A	B	L	E		I	R	O	N	W	O	R	K
	O				A		U		L		T	
C	A	T	A	C	L	Y	S	M	I	C		
	T		L						N		I	
		D	I	S	C	H	A	R	G	I	N	G
	B		G		O		P				K	
T	R	A	N	Q	U	I	L		F	A	W	N
	I		I		N		O		O		E	
U	N	K	N	O	T		M	A	N	G	L	E
	E		G		Y		B		D		L	

Favorite dish: MEATLOAF

PUZZLE 190

	T		H		S			
T	H	R	E	S	H	E	D	
	O		W	H	O		I	
H	U	T		A	R	M	S	
	S		O	P	T	I	C	
S	A	D		E	S	S	O	
	N		A			T		
	D	R	U	N	K		C	
U	S	E	S		A	W	E	
		S	T	A	Y	I	N	
A	N	T	I		A	F	T	
		S	N	A	K	E	S	

Thanksgiving dish: TURKEY

PUZZLE 191

Dinah the diner, skewer, kitchen

PUZZLE 192

	V	O	Y	A	G	E	S		I	D	E	A
Q		L		I		N		A		R		X
U	N	D	I	D		C	O	N	J	U	R	E
A			E		O		G		N			S
S	C	A	L	D	E	D		O	A	K	S	
H		L			E		R		A		T	
E	U	L	O	G	Y		F	A	I	R	E	R
S		O		I		W			D		A	
	S	T	A	G		I	M	P	O	S	E	D
U		M		G		L		R				I
S	H	E	L	L	E	D		A	C	O	R	N
E		N		Y		E		W		D		G
R	O	T	S		B	R	O	N	Z	E	D	

SELL LIKE HOTCAKES

PUZZLE 193

	J		K		P	A	R		A		S	
P	A	G	O	D	A		E	X	T	E	N	D
	G		H		N		A		O		E	
F	U	L	L	S	T	O	P		M	E	E	K
	A		R		R		E				Z	
T	R	E	A	T	Y		D	U	C	K	E	D
A		B						U				U
R	E	L	I	S	H		S	E	C	O	N	D
X			I		Y		Y		U		U	
A	P	E	D		R	O	S	E	M	A	R	Y
E		U		I		T		B		S		
S	C	R	E	E	N		E	L	E	V	E	N
	T		T		G	Y	M		R		D	

Tex-Mex dish: BURRITO

SOLUTIONS

PUZZLE 194

1. Whipped cream flavored with vanilla and sweetened.
2. This means cooked in greaseproof paper bags, but foil is a modern equivalent.
3. It is made by pouring a rich batter over fruit (often cherries) and baking.
4. Pumpkin.
5. Raspberries.
6. Tomatoes.
7. Stir in a little flour.
8. A fear of cooking.

PUZZLE 195

1. Cheese 2. Pepper 3. Olives
4. Shrimp 5. Tomato 6. Onions

PUZZLE 197

P	R	O	F	I	T		M	O	R	B	I	D
	E		L		H		I		U		N	
A	V	I	A	T	R	I	X		M	A	T	E
	E		T		I		E		B		R	
G	R	I	T		V	E	R	B	A	T	I	M
	E		E		E						N	
S	N	O	R	E	D		T	H	R	U	S	T
	T						H		E		I	
H	I	G	H	W	I	R	E		P	A	C	T
	A		E		N		O		A		A	
F	L	A	N		A	B	R	U	P	T	L	Y
	L		N		P		E		E		L	
T	Y	R	A	N	T		M	A	R	T	Y	R

Vegetable: EGGPLANT

PUZZLE 198

W		V		S		R
D	I	V	O	R	C	E	E
	S		W		A		A
	H	A	S	S	L	E	D
	X		C	L	A	Y
F	E	E		R	O	T
	M		L	A	P	S	E
F	O	X		W		N
	T		P	L	A	T	E
S	I	Z	E		F	U	R
	O		T	W	A	N	G
K	N	E	E		R	A	Y

Cracker: PRETZEL

PUZZLE 200

1. Recipe 2. Picnic 3. Course 4. Ration
5. Simmer 6. Buffet

PUZZLE 202

PORK, CORK, CORE, CARE, CAME, LAME, LAMB

PUZZLE 204

U		D		S		I		N		I		G
S	P	U	R	T	E	D		A	U	D	I	O
U		O		R		E		U		L		O
R	O	D	E	O		A	S	S	A	Y	E	D
P		E		L				E				B
	U	N	P	L	E	A	S	A	N	T	L	Y
A		U				P				A		E
D	E	M	O	N	S	T	R	A	B	L	E	
V				Y				S		L		R
I	N	S	U	L	A	R		S	T	Y	L	E
S		I		O		A		A		I		A
E	A	T	E	N		G	R	I	N	N	E	D
D		E		S		E		L		G		Y

Shellfish: OYSTER

SOLUTIONS

PUZZLE 205

Cheese: MONTEREY JACK

PUZZLE 207

LIKE PEAS IN A POD

PUZZLE 208

Type of pasta: MACARONI

PUZZLE 209

1. It is served flat and cut into wedges.
2. Cherries.
3. Grilling.
4. Onions.
5. Poached in red wine.
6. It becomes very tough.
7. Rice.
8. Chicken.

PUZZLE 210

The nine-letter word is MARINATED.

PUZZLE 211

There are 48 EGGS.

PUZZLE 212

Variety of soup: CORN CHOWDER

PUZZLE 213

Herb: OREGANO

SOLUTIONS

PUZZLE 215

SMELLS FISHY

PUZZLE 216

DOMINO'S PIZZA, WENDY'S, KRISPY KREME, TACO BELL, WETZEL'S PRETZELS, MCDONALD'S, LITTLE CAESARS, DOG N SUDS, PIZZA HUT, SONIC DRIVE-IN, SKIPPERS, BURGER KING, DUNKIN' DONUTS, PAPA JOHN'S, BIG BOY, WHITE CASTLE, ROCKY ROCOCO

PUZZLE 218

Snack food: POTATO CHIPS

PUZZLE 220

A	S	E	P	T	I	C		C	L	U	M	P
	K		E		D		H		E		A	
H	Y	D	R	O	E	L	E	C	T	R	I	C
	L		M		A		A				N	
P	A	R	A	L	L	E	L		C	O	L	D
	B		N			E		O		Y		
		D	E	P	E	N	D	E	N	T		
	R		N		L			C		A		
Q	U	I	T		U	N	S	E	E	I	N	G
	N			D		I		I		T		
I	N	E	F	F	E	C	T	I	V	E	L	Y
	E		A		D		A		E		E	
G	R	I	N	D		T	R	A	D	E	R	S

Name of a drink: ICED TEA

PUZZLE 221

MEAL, MEAT, MOAT, BOAT, BOOT, BOOK, COOK

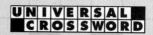

washingtonpost.com
Sunday Crossword

SUDOKU

Los Angeles Times
latimes.com
C R O S S W O R D

FREE
PUZZLE SOCIETY MEMBERSHIP
ACCESS TO THOUSANDS OF PUZZLES!

The Puzzle Society would like to thank you for your purchase by offering a free 90-day subscription to our online puzzle club. With this membership, you will have exclusive, unlimited access to 70+ updated puzzles added each week and 8,000+ archived puzzles.

To take advantage of this special membership offer, visit Puzzlesociety.com/play/lovers and start playing today!

The
Puzzle
Society™
puzzlesociety.com